To the Glory of Jesus Christ

who was born into this World as a little child and later gave His life on the Cross so that all who believe in Him may be saved

This Bible is Presented

To

Gloria Gelowitz

By

St. Peter C.W.L.

Through the Courtesy

of

The Harding Foundation • Raymondville, Texas

THE CATHOLIC BIBLE
IN PICTURES

VILLA NAZARETH
ROMA - VIA DELLA PINETA SACCHETTI, 29
TELEF. 569049

Mater orphanorum

Vatican City, May 18th,1956

Right Reverend and dear Monsignor,

I have met Mr. Sutliff, who presented me with a copy of the Bible which you have edited.

It is a nice volume, very interesting and very suitable for children. The boys of "Villa Nazareth" have already looked trough it with great interest, and it will be of great usefulness to them for the study of catechism and of religion in English.

With the sentiments of my high esteem and cordial regard, I remain

Yours sincerely in Christ

Domenico Tardini

Right Reverend
Monsignor DANTE DEL FIORENTINO
St.Lucy's Church
802 Kent Ave.
BROOKLYN 5,N.Y.

His Excellency, Msgr. Domenico Tardini, is Pro-Secretary of State at The Vatican.

So he arose and took the Child and His mother
and withdrew into Egypt.

[See page 18

THE CATHOLIC BIBLE IN PICTURES

EDITED BY

THE RIGHT REVEREND MONSIGNOR

DANTE DEL FIORENTINO

JOHN STEVENSON-PUBLISHER / NEW YORK • TORONTO • LONDON

Nihil Obstat: GEORGIUS DENZER, S.T.D., Censor Librorum

Imprimatur: ✠ THOMAS EDMUNDUS MOLLOY, S.T.D.,
Archiepiscopus-Episcopus Brooklyniensis

BROOKLYNII, Die XIX Decembris, 1955

THIS is a Bible Picture Book—with a difference. There are over a thousand illustrations with a simple text based on the Confraternity of Christian Doctrine Version, so designed that the Bible lives. The pictures are packed with action, and flow into one another in such a manner that the movement of the story is clearly seen. The whole is so presented that children as well as adults may see and understand.

The Catholic Church draws its inspiration from the eternal purpose of God revealed in the Bible, and in particular in its central figure, Our Lord and Savior Jesus Christ. But the Bible is a difficult book for the average person to read, and for two reasons: (1) We have been taught to take up a book and read it straight through, beginning at the first page and continuing to the last. The Bible does not lend itself easily to that method; it is a library rather than one book. (2) More and more we are being accustomed to see, and less and less are we able easily to grasp lengthy or involved and complicated reading.

So in this book we have selected the main stories of the Bible, and used the pages as a screen on which to project their movement; keeping, in the briefest possible captions, the essential parts of the story in language based on the Confraternity of Christian Doctrine Version, but tuned to our modern ear. There are three sections: "The Story of Jesus"; its background, "The Story of His People"; and its sequel, "The Story of His Church."

A number of persons have aided or advised the editor while this book was in preparation. Frederick Drimmer, M.A., editor-in-chief of The Greystone Press, gave freely of the wisdom of his long experience in the world of books; the Reverend George Denzer, S.T.D., of the Seminary of the Immaculate Conception at Huntington, Long Island, offered many illuminating, profoundly helpful suggestions; and the Reverend Felix Miritello assisted faithfully in the preparation of the manuscript. The editor wishes to express his most sincere indebtedness to them. Every care has been taken to make this book both accurate and memorable in its presentation.

The editor is indebted to the artists for the skill with which they have interpreted his suggestions, and the devotion and reverence with which they have undertaken their most difficult and delicate task.

I pray that this book may bring a fresh vision of Christ, and God's purpose in Him, to you who read it in the midst of the heartache and frustration of our modern world.

DANTE DEL FIORENTINO

225 PARK AVENUE SOUTH, NEW YORK, N.Y. 10003

LIBRARY OF CONGRESS CATALOG CARD NUMBER 55-10779

CONTENTS

PART I

THE STORY OF JESUS

PART II

THE STORY OF HIS PEOPLE

PART III

THE STORY OF HIS CHURCH

COLOR ILLUSTRATIONS BY HARRY COLLER AND KENNETH INNS
BLACK AND WHITE ILLUSTRATIONS BY ELSIE WALKER, DOUGLAS RELF, DESMOND WALDUCK, E. WALLCOUSINS, M. MACKINLAY, C. S. GOULD, MARJORIE WHITTINGTON, A. W. LACEY, SELBY DONNISON

PART I

The Story of Jesus

IN these pages you will see unfold before your eyes the greatest drama of all time. It is based upon the Gospels of Matthew, Mark, Luke and John—the first four books of the New Testament. Like countless numbers of men, women, and children before you, you will find it brings you courage and comfort, and lifts up your heart.

Here you will journey in strange and distant lands and be an eye-witness to marvelous happenings. With the wise men of the East you will follow a star to Bethlehem. You will watch the wondrous Child grow to wondrous Manhood. You will walk with Him and talk with Him, behold His kindly deeds of healing and consolation, and hear His message by the lake, on the hillside and in the city street. You will learn eternal truths about God and the life of man that will inspire and thrill you.

With the disciples you will sit in the Upper Room and partake of the Last Supper. You will make your way to the Mount of Olives and tarry in a garden called Gethsemani. You will stand amid the jostling Roman soldiery while Pilate sits in judgment, and you will walk the long way to Calvary. But in the garden of the empty tomb you will meet Him again, and on the mountain in Galilee, and there He will promise to be with you always.

The birth of a prophet

1. In the days of Herod, King of Judea——

2. —there lived a certain priest named Zachary and his wife, Elizabeth. Both were upright before God. They had no son, and were advanced in years.

3. The angel Gabriel appeared to Zachary in the Temple of the Lord and said, "Thy wife shall bear thee a son and thou shalt call him John."

4. Zachary said, "How shall I know this? For I am an old man and my wife is advanced in years." Gabriel replied, "Behold, thou shalt be unable to speak until these things come to pass." And when Zachary came out of the Temple he could not speak.

5. Elizabeth's time was fulfilled and she brought forth a son. Her neighbors and kinsfolk rejoiced with her. They were going to call him by his father's name, Zachary.

6. But his mother answered, "Not so, but he shall be called John." They said to her, "None of thy kindred is called by this name."

7. They kept inquiring of his father what he would have him called. And, asking for a writing-tablet, Zachary wrote the words, "John is his name."

8. Immediately Zachary's mouth was opened and he began to speak, blessing God. And he said to the child:

9. "Thou shalt go before the Lord to prepare His ways." And the child grew and was in the deserts.

Tidings for Mary

1. The angel Gabriel was sent from God to Nazareth to a virgin betrothed to Joseph, of the House of David. The virgin's name was Mary.

2. The angel said, "Hail, full of grace. Thou shalt bring forth a Son and thou shalt call Him Jesus, the Son of the Most High." Mary answered:

3. "Behold the handmaid of the Lord; be it done to me according to thy word." The angel departed and Mary went to the house of Zachary and greeted Elizabeth.

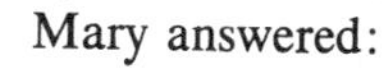

4. Elizabeth was filled with the Holy Spirit and cried, "Blessed art thou—blessed is the fruit of thy womb!" And Mary said:

My soul magnifies the Lord, and my spirit rejoices in God My Savior;

Because He has regarded the lowliness of His handmaid; for, behold, henceforth all generations shall call me blessed;

Because He who is mighty has done great things for me, and holy is His name;

And His mercy is from generation to generation on those who fear Him.

He has shown might with His arm, He has scattered the proud in the conceit of their heart.

He has put down the mighty from their thrones and has exalted the lowly.

He has filled the hungry with good things, and the rich He has sent away empty.

He has given help to Israel, His servant, mindful of His mercy—even as He spoke to our fathers—to Abraham and to his posterity forever.

5. In those days a decree went forth from Caesar Augustus, the Roman Emperor, that a census of the whole world should be taken.

6. And all were going, each to his own town, to register. Joseph went from Galilee out of the town of Nazareth into Judea to the town of David, which is called Bethlehem—because he was of the house and family of David—to register, together with Mary, his espoused wife, who was with child.

7. While they were there, the days for her to be delivered were fulfilled. And she brought forth her firstborn Son and wrapped Him in swaddling clothes, and laid Him in a manger, because there was no room for them in the inn.

The shepherds hear the news

1. There were shepherds in the same district living in the fields and keeping watch over their flock by night.

2. And behold, an angel of the Lord stood by them and said, "Do not be afraid, for I bring you good news of great joy. Today in the town of David a Savior has been born, Who is Christ the Lord. And this shall be a sign to you:

3. "You will find an Infant wrapped in swaddling clothes, lying in a manger." Suddenly there was a multitude of the heavenly host saying, "Glory to God in the highest, and on earth peace among men of good will."

4. The shepherds said one to another, "Let us go to Bethlehem." They went with haste, and found Mary and Joseph, and the Babe lying in the manger.

5. And when they had seen, they understood what had been told them concerning this Child. All who heard marveled at the things told them by the shepherds. The shepherds returned, glorifying and praising God.

The wise men seek the child

1. Behold, Magi came from the East to Jerusalem, saying, "Where is He that is born King of the Jews? We have seen His star and have come to worship Him."

2. But when King Herod heard this, he was troubled. He summoned the Magi and, sending them to Bethlehem, he said, "Go and make careful inquiry concerning the Child, and when you have found Him, bring me word, that I too may go and worship Him."

Jesus worked with Joseph as a carpenter and advanced in wisdom and grace before God and men.

[See page 22

He saw the Spirit of God descending as a dove
and coming upon Him . . .

[*See page* 23

"Lord, save me!" Peter cried when he began to sink.

[*See page* 63

"Who do you say I am?" "Thou art the Christ, the Son of the Living God!"

[*See page* 66

"Blessed is He Who comes as King in the name of the Lord," they said.

[See page 112

"Judas, dost thou betray the Son of Man with a kiss?"

[*See page* 137

"Dost Thou not know that I have power to crucify Thee?" said Pilate

[*See page* 144

He said to Thomas, "Bring here thy finger and see My hands . . ."

[See page 156

3. Now they went their way. And behold, the star they had seen in the East went before them, until it came and stood over the place where the Child was.

4. When they saw the star, they rejoiced. And entering the house, they found the Child with Mary, His mother, and, falling down, they worshipped Him. Opening their treasures, they offered Him gifts of gold, frankincense, and myrrh.

5. And being warned in a dream not to return to Herod, they went back to their country by another way.

The flight into Egypt

1. An angel appeared in a dream to Joseph, saying, "Take the Child and flee into Egypt, and remain there until I tell thee. For Herod will seek to destroy Him." So he arose and took the Child and His mother and withdrew into Egypt.

2. Herod, seeing that he had been tricked by the Magi, was exceedingly angry; and he sent and slew all the boys in Bethlehem and all its neighborhood who were two years old or under.

3. Then was fulfilled what was spoken through Jeremias the prophet: "A voice was heard in Rama, weeping and loud lamentation: Rachel weeping for her children."

4. When Herod was dead, an angel of the Lord appeared to Joseph, saying, "Go into the land of Israel, for those who sought the Child's life are dead."

5. So he arose and took the Child and His mother, and went into Israel. But hearing that Archelaus was reigning in Judea in place of his father, Herod, he was afraid to go there; being warned in a dream, he withdrew into the region of Galilee.

6. And he went and settled in a town called Nazareth, that there might be fulfilled what was spoken through the prophets: "He shall be called a Nazarene." And the Child grew and became strong. He was full of wisdom, and the grace of God was upon Him.

Jesus and the Rabbis

1. His parents were wont to go every year to Jerusalem——

2. —at the Feast of the Passover. And when He was twelve years old, they went up to Jerusalem according to the custom of the feast. When they were returning, the boy Jesus remained in Jerusalem, but His parents did not know it.

3. Thinking that He was in the caravan, they had come a day's journey before it occurred to them to look for Him among their relatives and acquaintances. And not finding Him, they returned to Jerusalem in search of Him.

4. After three days they found Him in the Temple, sitting in the midst of the teachers, both listening to them and asking them questions. All who were listening to Him were amazed at His understanding and His answers.

5. His mother said, "Son, why hast Thou done so to us? Thy father and I have been seeking Thee sorrowing." And He said, "Did you not know that I must be about My Father's business?" And they did not understand the word that He spoke to them.

6. He went with them to Nazareth, and was subject to them; and His mother kept all these things carefully in her heart. Jesus worked with His father as a carpenter, and advanced in wisdom and grace before God and men.

The baptism of Jesus

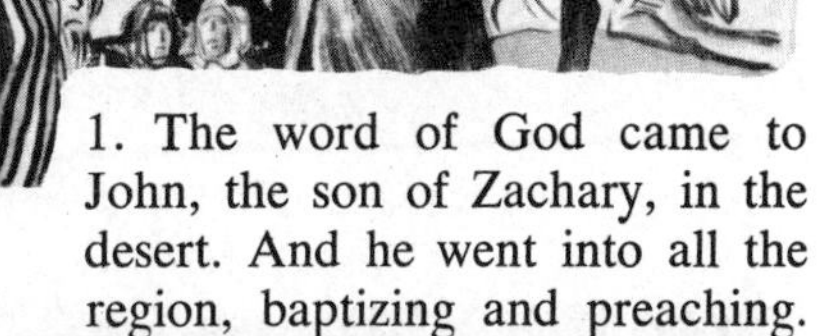

1. The word of God came to John, the son of Zachary, in the desert. And he went into all the region, baptizing and preaching.

2. Then Jesus came from Galilee to John, at the Jordan, to be baptized by him. John was for hindering Him and said:

3. "It is I who ought to be baptized by Thee, and dost Thou come to me?" But Jesus answered, "Let it be."

4. When Jesus had been baptized, the heavens were opened, and He saw the Spirit of God descending as a dove and coming upon Him. And behold, a voice from the heavens said, "This is My beloved Son, in Whom I am well pleased."

The temptation of Jesus

1. Then Jesus was led into the desert by the Spirit, to be tempted by the devil. And after fasting forty days and forty nights, He was hungry.

2. The tempter came and said to Him, "If Thou art the Son of God, command that these stones become loaves of bread."

3. But He answered, "It is written, 'Not by bread alone does man live, but by every word that comes forth from the mouth of God.' "

4. Then the devil set Him on the pinnacle of the Temple, and said, "If Thou art the Son of God, throw Thyself down; angels shall bear Thee up."

5. Jesus said to him, "It is written, 'Thou shalt not tempt the Lord thy God.'" Again, the devil took Him to a very high mountain, and showed Him all the kingdoms of the world and the glory of them.

6. And he said to Him, "All these things will I give Thee, if Thou wilt fall down and worship me." Then Jesus said to him, "Begone, Satan! for it is written, 'The Lord thy God shalt thou worship and Him only shalt thou serve.'" Then the devil left Him; and behold, angels came and ministered to Him.

Jesus calls his first disciples

1. The first followers of Jesus came to Him in this way.

2. John the Baptist was standing, and two of his disciples, Andrew and John. And looking upon Jesus as He walked by, he said, "Behold the Lamb of God!"

3. The two disciples followed Jesus and asked Him, "Rabbi, where dwellest Thou?" "Come and see," He replied. But Andrew first went to his brother Simon. "We have

4. The next day He found Philip. And Jesus said to him, "Follow Me."

5. Philip told Nathanael, "We have found the Messias in Jesus of Nazareth."

found the Christ!" he cried, and he led him to Jesus. Looking upon him, Jesus said, "Simon, thou shalt be called 'Peter' "— meaning a "rock."

6. But Nathanael replied, "Can anything good come out of Nazareth?" Philip said to him, "Come and see."

7. When Jesus told him, "Before Philip called thee, when thou wast under the fig tree, I saw thee," Nathanael answered, "Rabbi, Thou art the Son of God."

The first miracle of Jesus

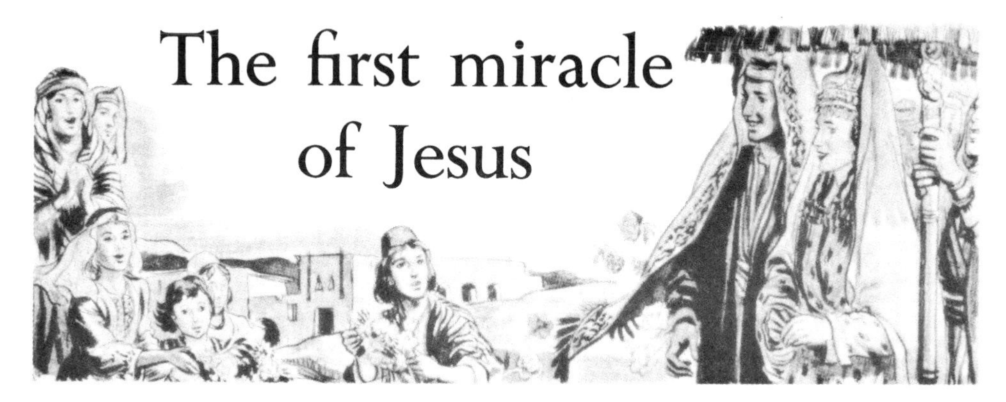

1. A marriage took place at Cana of Galilee, and the mother of Jesus was there. Now Jesus too was invited to the marriage, and also His disciples.

2. The wine having run short, the mother of Jesus said to Him, "They have no wine." "What wouldst thou have Me do?" Jesus asked. "My hour has not yet come."

3. His mother said to the attendants, "Do whatever He tells you." "Fill the jars with water," Jesus said to them. And they filled them to the brim.

4. Jesus said, "Draw out now." The chief steward tasted the water after it had become wine. Not knowing whence it was, he called the bridegroom and said, "Thou hast kept the good wine until now." This first of His signs Jesus worked at Cana.

Nicodemus

1. When He was at Jerusalem for the Passover feast, Nicodemus, a leader of the Jews, came to Jesus at night, and said, "Rabbi, we know Thou hast come as a teacher from God, for no one can work these signs that Thou workest unless God be with him."

2. Jesus answered, "Unless a man be born again, he cannot see the Kingdom of God." Nicodemus said, "How can a man be born when he is old?" Jesus answered, "Unless a man be born again of water and the Spirit he cannot enter into the Kingdom of God."

The woman by the well

1. Jesus left Judea and went again into Galilee. Now He came to a town of Samaria called Sichar. Wearied, Jesus sat down by the well.

2. There came a woman to draw water and Jesus asked her for a drink. The woman was startled, for Jews did not associate with Samaritans.

3. When He told her of her past life, she said, "I see Thou art a prophet, and I know the Messias is coming." Jesus answered, "I am He."

4. The woman went into town and said to the people, "Come and see a man who has told me all I have done. Can he be the Christ?" They came to Him.

5. They besought Him to stay; and He stayed two days. Far more believed because of His word. And they said, "This is in truth the Savior of the world."

The nobleman's son

1. After two days He departed from that place and went into Galilee, to Cana. The Galileans received Him, having seen all that He had done in Jerusalem during the feast.

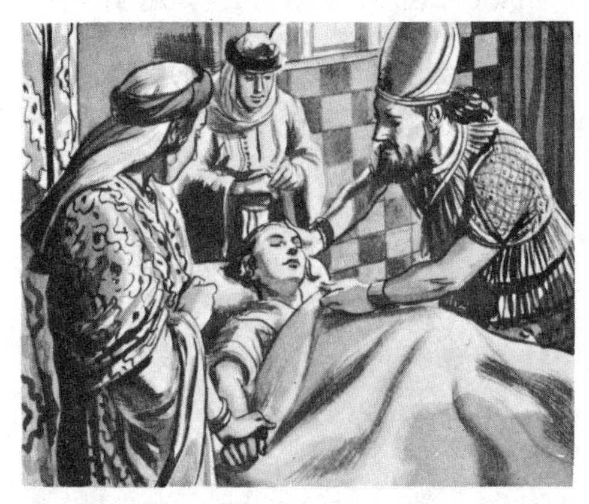

2. A royal official whose son was lying sick at Capharnaum heard Jesus had come and besought Him to heal his son, for he was at the point of death.

3. Jesus said to him, "Go thy way, thy son lives." The man believed the word that Jesus spoke to him and departed. But even as he was going——

4. —his servants met him and brought word saying that his son lived. He asked of them the hour in which he had got better.

5. They told him, "Yesterday, at the seventh hour, the fever left him." It was at that very hour Jesus said to him, "Thy son lives."

The miracle at Bethsaida

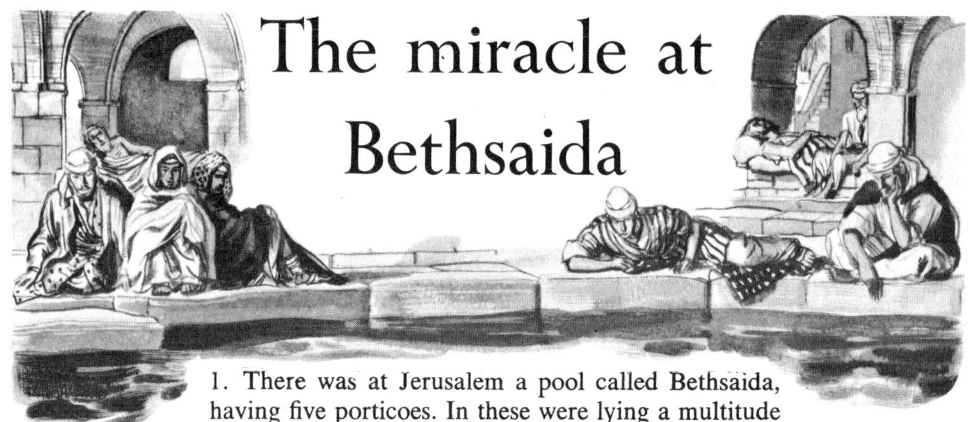

1. There was at Jerusalem a pool called Bethsaida, having five porticoes. In these were lying a multitude of the sick, waiting. For an angel used to come down at times into the pool. And the first to go into the pool, after the troubling of the water, was cured.

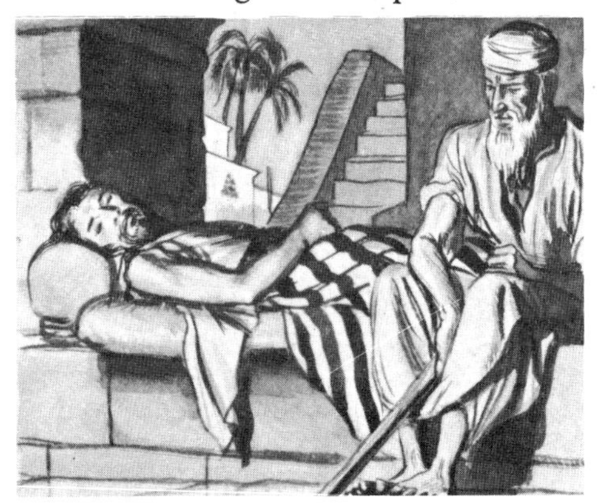

2. A certain man was there who had been thirty-eight years under his infirmity. Jesus saw him lying there. He said to him, "Dost thou want to get well?"

3. The sick man answered, "Sir, I have no one to put me into the pool when the water is stirred." "Rise, take up thy pallet and walk," Jesus said.

4. At once the man was cured. He took up his pallet and walked. But the priests rebuked him for carrying it on the Sabbath.

5. "I was told to do so," he replied. He did not know Jesus' name, but later, in the Temple, pointed Him out to the priests.

Nazareth rejects Jesus

1. When John the Baptist was imprisoned for denouncing Herod Antipas' marriage to his brother's wife——

2. —Jesus came to Nazareth. He entered the synagogue on the Sabbath and stood up to read, "The Spirit of the Lord is upon Me; because He has anointed Me to bring good news to the poor, the blind, the oppressed." Closing the volume, He began to say, "Today this Scripture has been fulfilled in your hearing."

3. All marveled, and they said, "Is not this Joseph's son?" Jesus said to them, "No prophet is acceptable in his own country." And all in the synagogue, as they heard these things, were filled with wrath. They rose up and put Him forth out of the town.

4. They led Him to the brow of the hill on which their town was built, that they might throw Him down headlong. But He, passing through their midst, went His way. And He went to Capharnaum, a town of Galilee.

"Fishers of men"

1. In Capharnaum He saw Simon and Andrew casting a net into the sea.

2. Getting into one of the boats, Simon's, He began to teach the crowds. When He had ceased, He said to Simon, "Put out into the deep, and lower your nets."

3. Simon answered, "The whole night we have toiled and taken nothing; but I will lower the net." And when they had, they enclosed a great number of fishes.

4. Simon and all who were with him were amazed at the catch of fish. Jesus said to Simon, "Do not be afraid; henceforth thou shalt catch men." And when they had brought their boats to land, they left all and followed Him.

The divine healer

1. At Capharnaum, He was teaching on the Sabbath. They were astonished, for His word was with authority.

2. In the synagogue a man possessed by an unclean devil cried out, "I know who Thou art, the Holy One of God." Jesus rebuked the devil, saying, "Hold thy peace, and go out of him." And the devil went out of him, without harming him at all.

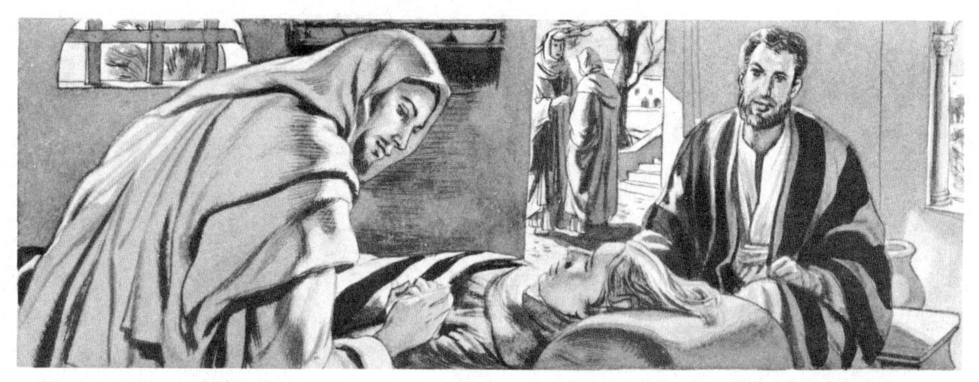

3. Jesus rose from the synagogue and entered Simon's house. Now Simon's mother-in-law was suffering from a great fever. Standing over her, He rebuked the fever, and it left her: she rose at once and began to wait on them.

4. Now when the sun was setting, all who had relatives sick with various diseases brought them to Him. And He laid His hands upon each of them and cured them. And they kept coming to Him from every direction.

The sermon on the mount

Seeing the crowds, He went up a mountain and taught them, saying:

"Blessed are the poor in spirit, for theirs is the Kingdom of Heaven.

"Blessed are the meek, for they shall possess the earth.

"Blessed are they who mourn, for they shall be comforted.

"Blessed are they who hunger and thirst for justice,
for they shall be satisfied.

"Blessed are the merciful, for they shall obtain mercy.

"Blessed are the pure of heart, for they shall see God.

"Blessed are the peacemakers, for they shall be called children of God.

"Blessed are they who suffer persecution for justice' sake,
for theirs is the Kingdom of Heaven.

"Blessed are you when men reproach you, and persecute you, and, speaking falsely,
say all manner of evil against you, for My sake.

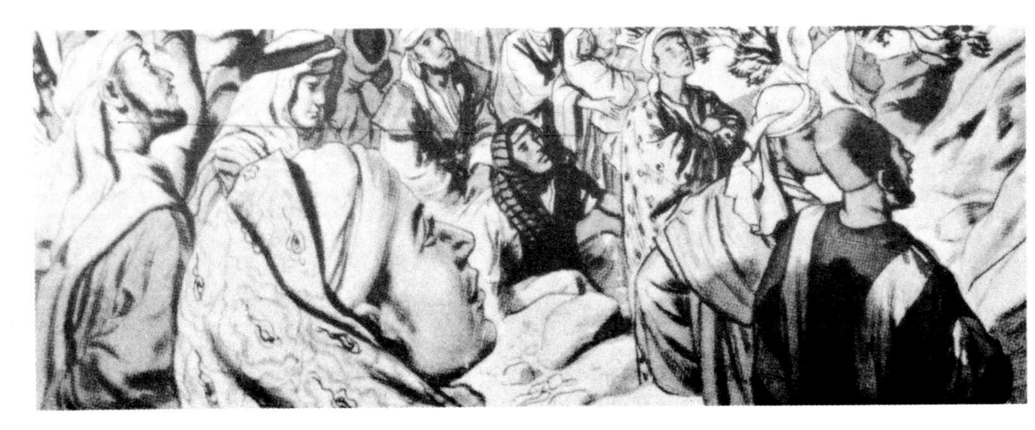

"Rejoice and exult,

because your reward is great in heaven; for so did they

persecute the prophets who were before you.

"In this manner shall you pray:

"Our Father Who art in heaven,

hallowed be Thy name.

"Thy kingdom come,

Thy will be done

on earth, as it is in heaven.

"Give us this day our daily bread.

"And forgive us our debts as we also forgive our debtors.

"And lead us not into temptation, but deliver us from evil."

Jesus heals a leper

1. Rising before daybreak, He went into a desert place and prayed. Simon, and those with him, followed. They found Him and said, "They are all seeking Thee."

2. And He said to them, "Let us go into the neighboring villages and towns, that there also I may preach."

3. There came to Him a leper, entreating Him; kneeling down, he said, "If Thou wilt, Thou canst make me clean."

4. Jesus stretched forth His hand, touched him, and said, "I will; be clean." At once the leprosy left him.

5. Then He strictly charged him, "See that thou tell no one." But he went and began to spread abroad the fact.

A cripple and his friends

1. Jesus again entered Capharnaum and was at home. Some men came, bringing a paralytic. Since they could not bring him to Jesus because of the crowd, they stripped off the roof and, having made an opening, let down the pallet on which the paralytic was lying.

2. Jesus said to the paralytic, "Thy sins are forgiven." But the Scribes began to argue, "Who can forgive sins but God?"

3. Jesus said to them, "The Son of Man has power to forgive sins." Then, to the paralytic, He said, "Arise." And he arose.

The disciple Matthew

1. He went forth and saw a tax-collector named Matthew in the tax-collector's place.

2. And He said to him, "Follow Me." And leaving all things, Matthew arose and followed Him.

3. Matthew gave a feast for Him, and a great gathering of tax-collectors were at the table with them.

4. The Pharisees and their Scribes grumbled to His disciples, "Why do you eat and drink with those who collect taxes for the Roman oppressors?"

5. "It is not the healthy who need a physician," Jesus answered, "but they who are sick. I have not come to call the just, but sinners, to repentance."

The true religion

1. Jesus went through standing grain, and His disciples plucked and ate some. The Pharisees said, "Why are you doing what is not lawful on the Sabbath?"

2. Jesus answered them, "The Son of Man is Lord even of the Sabbath." On another Sabbath He entered the synagogue and taught. A man was there and his right hand was withered. The Pharisees were watching whether He cured on the Sabbath, that they might accuse Him.

3. But He knew their thoughts and said to them, "Is it lawful on the Sabbath to do good?" He said to the man, "Stretch forth thy hand."

4. And he stretched it forth and his hand was restored. But they were filled with fury and began to discuss what they should do to Jesus.

Jesus chooses His twelve apostles

1. Now He went out to the mountain to pray, and continued all night in prayer to God. And when day broke, He summoned His disciples; and from these He chose twelve (whom He also named apostles): Simon, whom He named Peter, and his brother Andrew; James and John; Philip and Bartholomew; Matthew and Thomas; James, the son of Alpheus; Simon, called the Zealot; Thaddeus, the brother of James; and Judas Iscariot, who turned traitor. Having summoned the twelve apostles, He gave them power over all the devils, and to cure diseases.

2. He sent them forth to preach the Kingdom of God, and to heal the sick. And He said to them, "Take nothing for your journey, neither staff, nor wallet, nor bread, nor money; neither have two tunics. And whatever house you enter, stay there, and do not leave the place. And whoever does not receive you—go forth from that town, and shake off even the dust from your feet for a witness against them." And, going forth, they went about from village to village, preaching the gospel and working cures everywhere.

A Roman's faith

1. He entered Capharnaum. Now a servant of a certain centurion was sick to the point of death. The centurion, hearing of Jesus——

2. —sent to Him elders of the Jews, beseeching Him to come and save his servant. When they came to Jesus, they entreated Him, saying, "The officer is worthy, for he built our synagogue." So Jesus went with them. When He was not far from the house——

3. —the centurion sent friends to say, "I am not worthy that Thou shouldst come under my roof. But say the word, and my servant will be healed." Jesus marveled, and said, "Not even in Israel——

4. —have I found so great a faith." When the messengers returned to the house they found the servant in good health.

The widow's son

1. Afterwards He went to a town called Naim. A dead man was being carried out, the only son of a widow.

2. A large gathering was with her. The Lord, seeing her, had compassion, and said to her, "Do not weep."

3. He went up and touched the stretcher, and the bearers stood still. He said, "Young man, I say to thee, arise."

4. He who was dead sat up, and began to speak. And He gave him to his mother. But fear seized upon all, and they began to glorify God; saying, "A great prophet has risen among us," and "God has visited His people." This report concerning Him went forth throughout the whole of Judea, and all the country roundabout.

Jesus rebukes a Pharisee

1. One of the Pharisees asked Him to dine with him; so He went into the house and reclined at the table.

2. A woman in the town, who was a sinner, brought an alabaster jar of ointment. Standing behind Him, she began to bathe His feet with her tears, and wiped them with the hair of her head, and kissed His feet, and anointed them with ointment.

3. When the Pharisee saw it, he said to himself, "This Man, were He a prophet, would surely know what manner of woman is touching Him, for she is a sinner." Jesus answered him, "Simon, I have something to say to thee." And he said, "Master, speak." "A certain money-lender had two debtors; one owed five hundred denarii, the other fifty. As they had no means of paying, he forgave them both. Which will love him more?" Simon answered, "He, I suppose, whom he forgave more." And He said, "Thou hast judged rightly." Turning to the woman, He said to Simon, "Dost thou see this woman? I came into thy house; thou gavest Me no water for My feet; but she has bathed My feet with tears, and wiped them with her hair. Thou gavest Me no kiss, but she, from the moment she entered, has not ceased to kiss My feet; she has anointed My feet with ointment. Her sins, many as they are, shall be forgiven, because she has loved much."

4. And He said to her, "Thy sins are forgiven." They who were at table with Him began to say within themselves, "Who is this Man, who even forgives sins?" But He said to the woman, "Thy faith has saved thee; go in peace."

He cures a dumb man

1. There was brought to Him a possessed man who was blind and dumb, and He cured him so that he spoke and saw. And the crowds marveled.

2. The Scribes, who had come down from Jerusalem, said, "He has Beelzebub," and "By the prince of devils He casts out devils." But He called them together, and said to them in parables, "How can Satan cast out Satan? A house divided against itself cannot stand.

3. "You say I cast out devils by Beelzebub. But if I cast out devils by the finger of God, then the Kingdom of God has come upon you. He who is not with Me is against Me. Whoever blasphemes against the Holy Spirit never has forgiveness."

His true family

1. Again a crowd gathered so that Jesus and the disciples could not so much as take their food. When His own family had heard of it, they went to lay hold of Him, for they said, "He has gone mad."

2. And His mother and His brethren came, and standing outside, they sent to Him, calling Him.

3. Now a crowd was sitting about Him and they said to Him, "Behold, Thy mother and Thy brethren are outside, seeking Thee."

4. He answered them, "Who are My Mother and My brethren?" And looking round on those who were sitting about Him, He said, "Behold My mother and My brethren. For whoever does the will of God, he is My brother and sister and mother."

The parable of the sower

1. Again He began to teach by the water's edge. As a great crowd gathered, He got into a boat. And He taught them in parables. He said:

2. "Behold, the sower went out to sow. And some seed fell by the wayside and the birds came and ate it up.

3. "Other seed fell upon rocky ground where it was scorched and withered away.

4. "Other seed fell among thorns; and the thorns grew up and choked it.

5. "Other seed fell upon good ground, and yielded fruit." The Twelve asked about the parable. He said, "The sower sows the Word."

The parable of the weeds

1. Another parable He set before them, saying:

2. "The Kingdom of Heaven is like a man who sowed good seed in his field; but while men were asleep——

3. "—his enemy came and sowed weeds among the wheat. When the blade sprang up, the weed appeared as well.

4. "The servants said, 'Wilt thou have us gather the weeds?' 'No,' he said, 'lest you root up the wheat with them.

5. " 'At harvest time, gather the weeds, and bind them in bundles to burn; but gather the wheat into my barn.' "

“The Kingdom of Heaven”

1. All these things Jesus spoke to the crowds in parables. His disciples came to him saying, “Explain the parable of the weeds.” So He said:

2. “The Kingdom of Heaven is like a treasure hidden in a field; he who finds it hides it, and sells all he has and buys that field.

3. “The Kingdom of Heaven is like a merchant in search of fine pearls. When he finds a pearl of great price, he sells all he has and buys it.

4. “The Kingdom of Heaven is like leaven, which a woman took and buried in flour until all of it was leavened.

5. “The Kingdom is like a net cast into the sea. When it was filled, they gathered the good, but threw away the bad.”

A storm at sea

1. He said, when evening had come, "Let us cross to the other side." He got into a boat, and His disciples followed.

2. There arose a great squall, and the waves were beating into the boat, so that the boat was now filling. He Himself was in the stern, on the cushion, asleep. They woke Him and said, "Master, does it not concern Thee that we are perishing?"

3. Rising up, He rebuked the wind, and said to the sea, "Peace, be still!" The wind fell and there came a great calm. And He said to the disciples, "Why are you fearful? Are you still without faith?" But they feared exceedingly and said to one another, "Who is this, that even the wind and the sea obey Him?"

The madman among the tombs

1. They came to the other side of the sea. There met Him from the tombs a man possessed by unclean spirits.

2. When he saw Jesus, he said, "Do not torment me!" Jesus asked him, "What is thy name?" "My name is legion, for we spirits are many."

3. A herd of swine was on the mountainside. The spirits kept entreating, "Send us into the swine." Jesus gave them leave, and the herd rushed into the sea.

4. The swineherds reported it in the town. People came to Jesus, and saw the man who had been afflicted, sitting clothed and in his right mind.

5. But they were afraid and asked Jesus to depart. The man wanted to go with Him, but Jesus said, "Go home and tell all that the Lord has done for thee."

The daughter of Jairus

1. Jesus crossed over in the boat to the other side, and a great crowd gathered. One of the rulers of the synagogue, Jairus, entreated Him, saying, "My daughter is at the point of death; come, lay Thy hands upon her, that she may live."

2. Jesus went with him, and a great crowd was following. A woman who for twelve years had had a hemorrhage came up behind and touched His cloak. For she said, "If I touch but His cloak I shall be saved." At once she was healed.

3. Jesus turned. "Who touched My cloak?" The woman, trembling, told Him. But He said, "Daughter, thy faith has saved thee. Go in peace." As He spoke——

4. —there came some from the house of the ruler of the synagogue, saying, "Thy daughter is dead." But Jesus said, "Do not be afraid, only have faith."

5. They came to the house of the ruler of the synagogue and He saw people weeping. Going in, He said to them, "Why do you make this din, and weep? The girl is asleep, not dead." And they laughed Him to scorn.

6. He took the father and mother and those who were with Him, and entered in where the girl was lying.

7. And taking the girl by the hand, He said to her, "Talitha cumi," which is interpreted, "Girl, I say to thee, arise."

8. The girl rose up immediately and began to walk; she was twelve years old. They were utterly amazed. And He charged them strictly that no one should know of it, and directed that something be given her to eat. But the report of this spread throughout all that district.

The death of John the Baptist

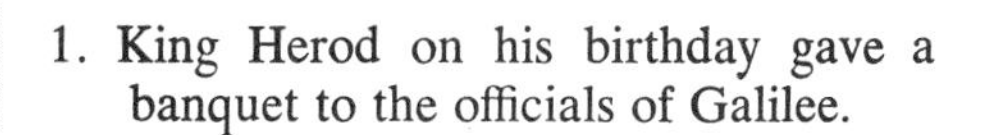

1. King Herod on his birthday gave a banquet to the officials of Galilee.

2. Salome, daughter of Herodias, his wife, danced for them and pleased Herod. The King swore to the girl, "Ask what thou willest, and I will give it to thee."

3. She said to her mother, "What am I to ask for?" "John the Baptist's head," Herodias answered. For John had condemned her for marrying her brother-in-law.

4. The King, hearing Salome's request, was grieved. But he had sworn an oath. He commanded that John be beheaded.

5. John's head was brought on a dish and the girl gave it to her mother. John's disciples took away his body.

Feeding the five thousand

1. Hearing of John's death, Jesus went to a desert place. But the crowds followed, and He cured their sick.

2. When evening came, His disciples wanted them to be sent away for food. "Feed them yourselves!" said Jesus. Andrew said, "This boy has five loaves and two fishes——

3. "—but what are these among so many?" "Bring them here to Me," He said. And He ordered the crowd to recline, for there was much grass in the place.

4. He took the loaves and fishes, blessed and broke them, and gave them to His disciples to set before the people. All ate and were satisfied; and they gathered up what was left—twelve baskets full. Those who had eaten were five thousand.

Jesus walks on the sea

1. When the people had seen the miracle, they said, "This is indeed the Prophet!" Jesus perceived they would come to take Him by force and make Him king.

2. But He would not have it so. He made His disciples get into the boat and cross the sea ahead of Him to Bethsaida, while He Himself dismissed the crowd. Then He went away to a mountain to pray. And when it was late, the ship was in the midst of the sea, and He alone on the land. Seeing them straining at the oars, for the wind was against them, about the fourth watch of the night He came to them, walking upon the sea. But they thought it was a ghost and cried out, for they all were troubled. Then He immediately said to them, "Take courage; it is I, do not be afraid."
But Peter answered:

3. "Lord, if it is Thou, bid me come to Thee over the water." "Come," He said.

4. Peter walked on the water. When he saw the strong wind, he was afraid; as he began to sink he cried, "Lord, save me!" Jesus took hold of him, saying:

5. "Why didst thou doubt?" When they got into the boat, the wind fell. They who were in the boat worshipped Him, saying, "Truly Thou art the Son of God."

Jesus in Phoenicia

1. Jesus departed with His disciples to the district of Tyre and Sidon, in Phoenicia. Here they stayed in secret, but a Canaanite woman came to the house and cried out, "Have pity on me, my daughter is sorely beset by a devil!"

2. Jesus answered, "I was not sent except to the lost sheep of the house of Israel." But she worshipped Him, saying, "Lord, help me!" He said in answer, "It is not fair to take the children's bread and to cast it to the dogs." This He said because He had come —

3. — to bring the Kingdom of God first to the children of Israel. .But she said, "Yes, Lord; for even the dogs eat of the crumbs that fall from their masters' table."

4. Then Jesus answered her, "O woman, great is thy faith! Let it be done to thee as thou wilt." And her daughter was healed from that moment.

The power that heals

1. From Tyre, He came to the sea of Galilee. And they brought to Him one deaf and dumb.

2. He put His fingers to the man's ears, and spitting, touched his tongue. Looking to heaven, He sighed, "Be opened."

3. And his ears were at once opened, and he began to speak correctly. And He charged them to tell no one.

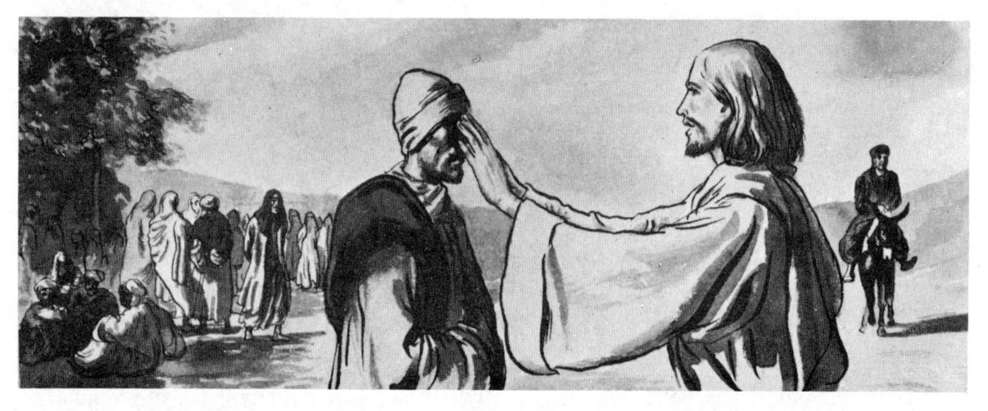

4. They came to Bethsaida and they brought Him a blind man. He led him outside the village; applying spittle to his eyes, He laid His hands upon him, and asked if he saw anything. The man said, "I see men as trees walking." Again He laid His hands upon the man's eyes, and he saw all things plainly.

Peter's confession of faith

1. Now Jesus, having come into the district of Caesarea Philippi, asked His disciples, "Who do men say I am?" "One of the prophets," they said. "Who do you say I am?"

2. Simon Peter answered, "Thou art the Christ, the Son of the living God." "Blessed art thou, Simon," answered Jesus.

3. "Flesh and blood has not revealed this to thee, but My Father in heaven. Thou art Peter, and on this rock I will build My Church, and the gates of hell shall not prevail against it. And I will give thee the keys of the Kingdom of Heaven." Then He charged His disciples to tell no one that He was Jesus the Christ.

4. Jesus began to show His disciples that He must go to Jerusalem and suffer many things from the Scribes and chief priests, and be put to death, and on the third day rise again. Peter began to chide, "Lord, this will never happen to Thee."

5. But He rebuked Peter, saying, "Get behind Me, Satan, for thou dost not mind the things of God, but those of men." Calling the crowd together, He said, "If anyone wishes to come after Me, let him take up his cross, and follow Me. He who loses his life for My sake and for the gospel's sake will save it."

The Transfiguration

After six days Jesus took Peter, James and John, and led them up a high mountain, off by themselves, and was transfigured before them. His face shone as the sun and His garments became white as snow. And there appeared to them Moses and Elias, the two great prophets, talking together with Him. Then Peter addressed Jesus, saying, "Lord, it is good for us to be here. Let us set up three tents, one for Thee, and one for Moses, and one for Elias." As he was still speaking, a bright cloud overshadowed them, and a voice out of the cloud said, "This is My beloved Son; hear Him." Suddenly looking round, they no longer saw anyone but Jesus.

"If you have faith"

1. When they came down from the mountain a man approached Him, saying, "Lord, have pity on my son, for he is a lunatic; often he falls into fire and into water. I brought him to Thy disciples, but they could not cure him." Jesus answered, "O, unbelieving generation, how long shall I be with you? Bring thy son to Me."

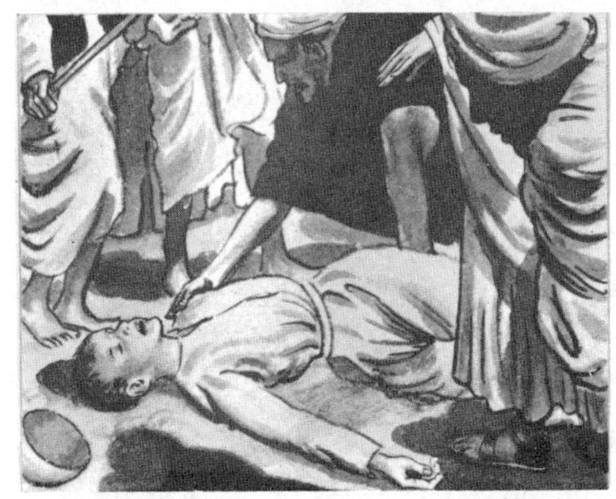

2. The boy fell down, foaming at the mouth. "All things are possible to him who believes," Jesus said. The father cried, "I believe; help my unbelief."

3. Jesus took the boy by the hand and he stood up. From that moment he was cured. And He said, "If you have faith, nothing will be impossible to you."

The greatest in God's Kingdom

1. Leaving that place, Jesus and His disciples passed through Galilee, and they came to Capharnaum. When He was at home, He asked them, "What were you arguing about on the way?" But they kept silence, for on the way they had discussed with one another——

2. —which of them was the greatest. And sitting down, He called the Twelve and said to them, "If any man wishes to be first, he shall be last of all, and servant of all." And Jesus called a little child to Him, and set him in the midst of them, and taking him into His arms, He said:

3. "Unless you turn and become like little children, you will not enter into the Kingdom of Heaven. Whoever humbles himself as this little child, he is the greatest in the Kingdom of Heaven. And whoever receives one such little child for My sake, receives Me; and whoever receives Me, receives not Me but Him who sent Me."

Jesus in the midst

After He had taught them this, Jesus told the disciples, "If two of you shall agree on earth about anything at all for which they ask, it shall be done for them by My Father in heaven. For where two or three are gathered together for My sake, there am I in the midst of them."

The ungrateful servant

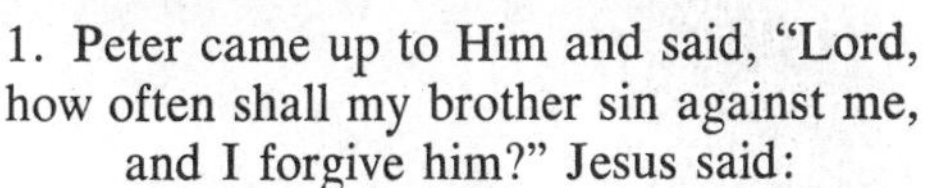

1. Peter came up to Him and said, "Lord, how often shall my brother sin against me, and I forgive him?" Jesus said:

2. "A king desired to settle accounts with his servants. One owed him ten thousand talents. The king ordered him sold, and all he had. But the servant begged, 'Have patience, I will pay thee!'

3. "Moved, the king forgave him the debt. But as that servant went out, he met one of his fellow-servants who owed him a hundred denarii. He laid hold of him, saying, 'Pay what thou owest.'

4. "His fellow-servant entreated him, 'Have patience, I will pay thee.' But he cast him into prison. The king, hearing of this, cried, 'Wicked servant, I forgave thy debt!'

5. "Angry, he handed him over to the torturers until he should pay. So My Heavenly Father will do to you, if you do not each forgive your brothers."

The thunderers

1. When the days had come for Him to be taken up, He steadfastly set His face to go to Jerusalem.

2. He sent messengers before Him. And they went and entered a Samaritan town to make ready for Him, but the people did not receive Him, because His face was set for Jerusalem. When His disciples James and John saw this, they said:

3. "Lord, wilt Thou that we bid fire come down from heaven and consume them?" But He turned and rebuked them, saying, "You do not know——

4. "—of what manner of spirit you are; for the Son of Man did not come to destroy men's lives, but to save them." And they went to another village.

The cost of discipleship

1. As they went on their journey, a man said to Him, "I will follow Thee wherever Thou goest." Jesus said to him, "The foxes have dens, and the birds of the air have nests, but the Son of Man has nowhere to lay His head."

2. Jesus said to another, "Follow Me." But he said, "Lord, let me first bury my father." Jesus answered, "Leave the dead to bury their own dead." Another said, "Let me first bid farewell to those at home." Jesus said to him, "No one, having put his hand to the plow and looking back, is fit for the Kingdom of God."

“The Light of the World”

1. The Feast of Tabernacles was at hand. His brethren said to Him, “Go into Judea——

2. “—Manifest Thyself to the world.” For not even His brethren believed. Jesus said, “You go, but I will not, for My time is not yet fulfilled.” But as soon as His brethren had gone, He also went, privately. He went into the Temple and began to teach.

3. Many believed in Him. Hearing the crowd whispering, the Pharisees sent attendants to seize Him. But no one laid hands on Him. The Pharisees said:

4. “Why have you not brought Him?” The attendants answered, “Never has man spoken as this Man.” “Have you also been led astray?” the Pharisees asked.

5. Jesus spoke these words, while teaching in the Temple: "I am the Light of the World. He who follows Me does not walk in the darkness, but will have the light of life. If any-one keep My word, he will never see death."

6. The Jews said, "Art Thou greater than our father Abraham, who is dead? And the prophets are dead. Whom dost Thou make Thyself out to be?" Jesus said to them, "Amen, amen, I say to you, before Abraham came to be, I am." They took up stones to cast at Him; but Jesus hid Himself, and went out from the Temple.

A sinful woman

1. The Scribes and Pharisees brought a sinful woman and said to Him, "Master, in the Law, Moses commanded us to stone such persons. What, therefore, dost Thou say?" Now they were saying this to test Him, in order that they might be able to accuse Him. But Jesus, stooping down, began to write with His finger on the ground.

2. When they continued asking Him, He said, "Let him who is without sin among you be the first to cast a stone." Ashamed, they went away, one by one.

3. Then Jesus said to the woman, "Has no one condemned thee?" "No one, Lord." "Neither will I condemn thee," Jesus said. "Go thy way, and sin no more."

The man born blind

1. Passing by, He saw a man blind from birth. Jesus made clay with spittle, spread the clay over his eyes, and said, "Wash in the pool of Siloe."

2. So he went away, washed, and returned seeing. The neighbors asked, "How were thy eyes opened?" When he told them, they took him to the Pharisees.

3. The Jews did not believe he had been blind until they called his parents and questioned them. "Who opened his eyes we do not know," his parents said.

4. They feared that if they confessed Jesus to be the Christ, they should be put out of the synagogue. But the Pharisees turned the son out because he said:

5. "If this Man were not from God, He could do nothing." Jesus found him and asked, "Dost thou believe in the Son of God?" "I believe, Lord!" he cried.

The Good Shepherd

1. Jesus said, "I came that they may have life, and have it more abundantly.

2. "I am the good shepherd. The good shepherd lays down his life for his sheep. But the hireling, who is not a shepherd, who does not own the sheep, sees the wolf coming and leaves the sheep and flees. And the wolf snatches and scatters the sheep; but the hireling flees—because he is a hireling, and has no concern for the sheep.

3. "I am the good shepherd, and I know Mine and Mine know Me, even as the Father knows Me and I know the Father; and I lay down My life for My sheep. Other sheep I have that are not of this fold.—

4. "Them also I must bring, and they shall hear My voice, and there shall be one fold and one shepherd. The Father loves Me because I lay down My life that I may take it up again. No one takes it from Me, but I lay it down of Myself."

The good Samaritan

1. A lawyer got up to test Him, saying, "Master, what must I do to gain eternal life?" Jesus asked him, "What is written in the Law?" "Thou shalt love God with thy whole heart, soul, strength, and mind, and thy neighbor as thyself," he answered.

2. "Do this and thou shalt live," Jesus said to him. "And who is my neighbor?" asked the lawyer. Jesus answered, "A man was going from Jerusalem to Jericho. He fell in with robbers, who, after stripping and beating him, went their way, leaving him half-dead.

3. "As it happened, a certain priest was going the same way, and when he saw the wounded man, he passed by.

4. "And likewise an assistant of the priests, when he was near the place and saw him, passed by.

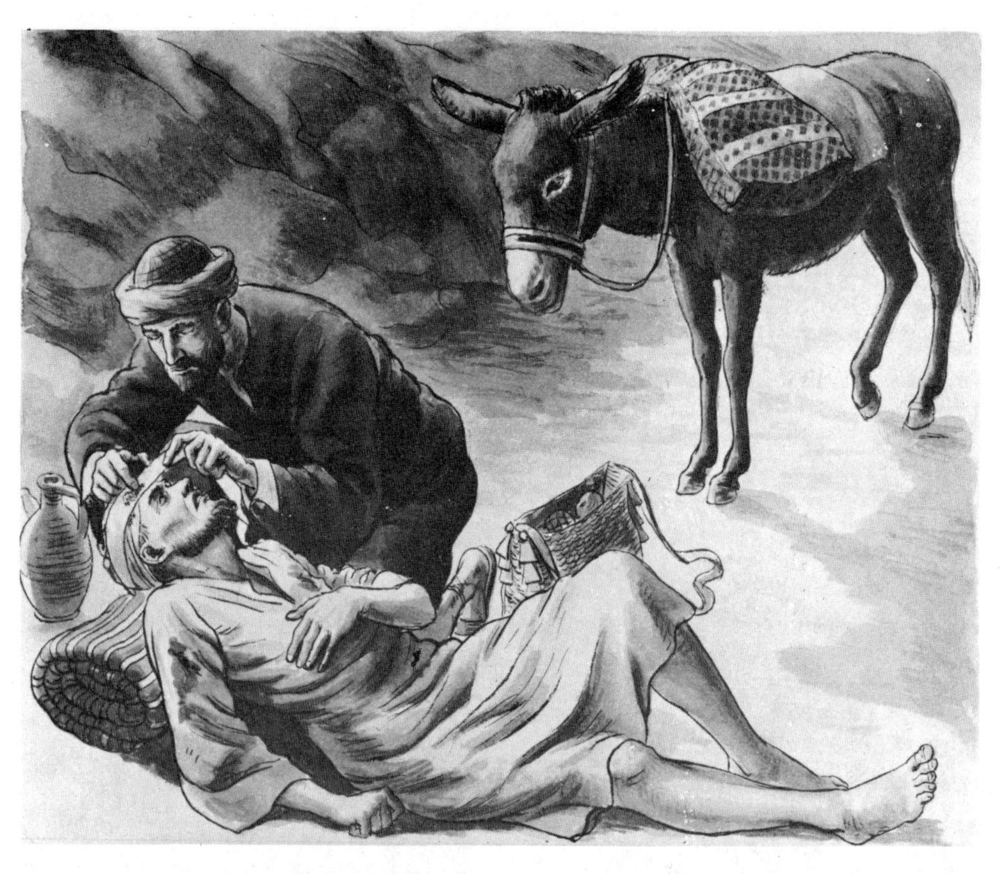

5. "But a certain Samaritan, as he journeyed, came upon him and was moved with compassion. He bound up his wounds, pouring on oil and wine. Setting him on his own beast, he brought him to an inn and took care of him.

6. "When he left, he told the innkeeper, 'Take care of him; and whatever thou spendest, I will repay thee.'

7. "Which proved himself neighbor?" asked Jesus. The lawyer replied, "He who took pity." "Go—and do the same," Jesus said.

Martha and Mary

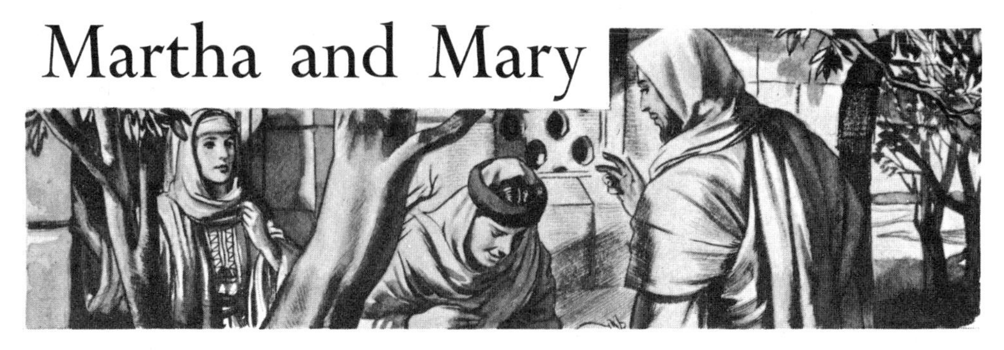

1. Jesus and His disciples entered Bethany, where a woman named Martha welcomed Him to her house. She had a sister, Mary, who sat down at the Lord's feet and listened to Him.

2. But Martha, busy about much serving, came up and said, "Lord, is it no concern of Thine that my sister has left me to serve alone? Tell her to help me." The Lord answered, "Martha, thou art anxious about many things, yet only one is needful. Mary has chosen the best part, and it will not be taken away from her."

The rich fool

1. "A man's life," said Jesus, "does not consist in the abundance of possessions." And He spoke a parable: "The land of a rich man brought forth more crops than he had room to store.

2. "And he thought, 'I will pull down my barns and build larger ones, and there I will store all my grains and my goods.

3. " 'And I will say to my soul: "Soul, thou hast many good things laid up for many years; take thy ease, eat, drink, be merry." '

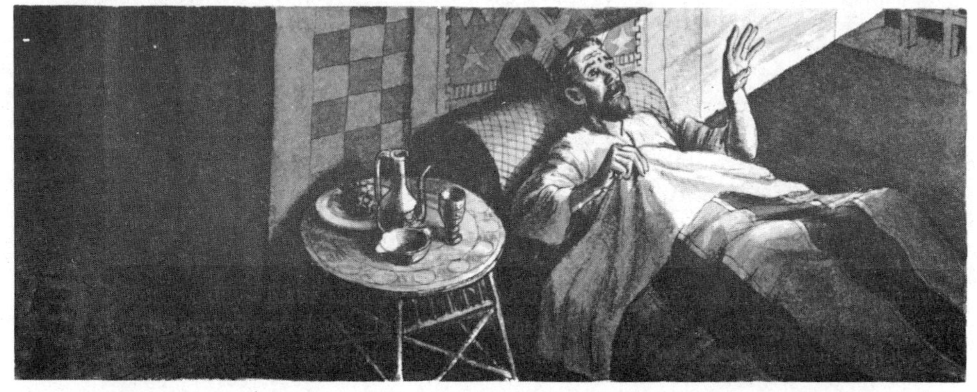

4. "But God said to him, 'Thou fool, this night do they demand thy soul of thee; and the things that thou hast provided, whose will they be?' " Then Jesus said to His disciples, "So is he who lays up treasure for himself, and is not rich as regards God. Therefore, I say to you, do not be anxious about life."

Worldly anxiety

"Look at the birds," Jesus taught again. "They do not sow, or reap, yet your Heavenly Father feeds them. Consider how the lilies of the field grow; they neither toil nor spin, yet not even Solomon in all his glory was arrayed like one of these. Therefore do not say, 'What shall we eat?' or 'What are we to put on?' Your Father knows you need these things. Seek first the Kingdom of God and His justice, and all these things shall be given to you."

Watching for the Master's coming

1. "Watch," said Jesus, "for you do not know at what hour your Lord is to come.

2. "Let your lamps be burning and you yourselves like men waiting for their master's return from a wedding, so that when he knocks they may straightway open to him. Blessed are those servants whom the master on his return shall find watching. I say to you, he will make them recline at table, and will come and serve them.

3. "Whom dost thou think the master will set over his household? That servant whom the master, when he comes, shall find giving the others their food in due time."

4. "But if that servant says, 'My master delays his coming,' and begins to beat the others and get drunk, the master will come unexpectedly and will cut him asunder."

Healing on the Sabbath

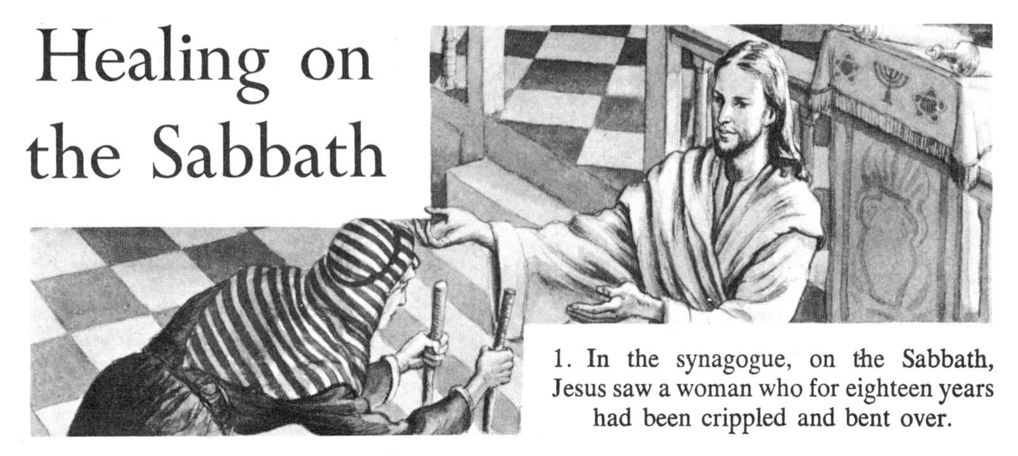

1. In the synagogue, on the Sabbath, Jesus saw a woman who for eighteen years had been crippled and bent over.

2. He laid His hands upon her. Instantly she was made straight, and glorified God. The ruler of the synagogue was indignant that Jesus had cured on the Sabbath. But the Lord said, "Does not each of you on the Sabbath loose his ox or ass, and lead it to water? And this woman—ought not she to be loosed from this bond on the Sabbath?"

"I and the Father are One"

1. Now there took place at Jerusalem the Feast of the Dedication, and it was winter. Jesus was walking in the Temple, in Solomon's porch. The Jews gathered round and said, "How long dost Thou keep us in suspense? If Thou art the Christ, tell us openly."

2. Jesus answered them, "I tell you and you do not believe. The works that I do in the name of My Father bear witness concerning Me. My sheep hear My voice, and they follow Me. They shall never perish, neither shall anyone snatch them out of My hand. No one is able to snatch anything out of the hand of My Father. I and the Father are One."

3. At once the Jews took up stones to stone Him. But Jesus answered, "Many good works have I shown you from My Father. For which do you stone Me?" They answered, "Not for a good work, but for blasphemy, because Thou, being a man, makest Thyself God!"

4. When they sought to seize Him, He escaped out of their hands. He went beyond the Jordan, to the place where John the Baptist first baptized, and there He stayed. Many came to Him and they believed in Him, saying, "John indeed worked no miracle; all things, however, that John said of this Man were true."

Lament over Jerusalem

1. Certain Pharisees came up, saying to Him, "Depart, for Herod wants to kill Thee." He answered:

2. "Go and say to that fox, I must go My way, today and tomorrow and the next day. It cannot be that a prophet should perish outside Jerusalem. Jerusalem, Jerusalem, thou who killest the prophets, and stonest those who are sent to thee! How often would I have gathered thy children together, as a hen gathers her young under her wings—but thou wouldst not!"

The true disciple

1. "Everyone of you who does not renounce all that he possesses," said Jesus, "cannot be My disciple. A certain man," He went on, "gave a great supper, and sent his servant to tell those invited to come. They all began to excuse themselves.

2. "The first said, 'I have bought a farm, and must go out and see it.'

3. "Another said, 'I have bought five yoke of oxen and am going to try them.'

4. "And another said, 'I have married a wife, and therefore I cannot come.'

5. "The servant reported these things. His master was angry and said, 'Go into the streets and lanes and bring in the poor, the crippled, the blind and the lame.'

6. "Still there was room. Then the master said, 'Go out into the highways and hedges and make them come. None of those who were invited shall taste my supper!"

7. Jesus asked His listeners, "Which of you, wishing to build a tower, does not sit down first and calculate whether he has the means to complete it? Lest all who behold begin to mock him, saying, 'This man began to build and was not able to finish!'

8. "Or what king, setting out for battle, does not first consider whether he is able to defeat the enemy?

9. "Or else, whilst the enemy is yet at a distance, he sends a delegation and asks the terms of peace."

10. Now great crowds were going along with Him. And He turned and said to them, "If anyone comes to Me and does not love Me more than his father and mother and wife and children, and brothers and sisters, yes, and even his own life, he cannot be My disciple. And he who does not carry his cross and follow Me, cannot be My disciple."

The lost sheep

1. When the Pharisees complained, "This Man welcomes sinners," Jesus answered, "There will be more joy in heaven over one sinner who repents, than over ninety-nine who have no need of repentance. What man of you, having a hundred sheep, and losing one——

2. "—does not leave the ninety-nine and go after that which is lost until he finds it? And when he has found it, he lays it upon his shoulders rejoicing.

3. "On coming home, he calls together his friends and neighbors, saying to them, 'Rejoice with me, because I have found my sheep that was lost.' "

The lost coin

1. To illustrate the same lesson in His teaching, Jesus spoke again by parable. "What woman, having ten pieces of silver," He said, "if she loses one, does not light a lamp and sweep the house and search carefully until she finds it?

2. "And when she has found it, she calls together her friends and neighbors, saying, 'Rejoice with me, for I have found the piece of silver that I had lost.' Even so," said Jesus to the Pharisees and Scribes who were listening, "there will be joy among the angels of God over one sinner who repents."

The lost son

1. Jesus said, "A certain man had two sons. The younger of them said, 'Father, give me the share of the property that is due to me.' The father divided his means between them.

2. "Not many days later, the younger son journeyed into a far country, and squandered his fortune in loose living.

3. "There came a famine over that country, and he began to suffer want. He went to one of the citizens——

4. "—who sent him to his farm to feed swine. But when he came to himself, he said, 'How many hired men in my father's house have bread in abundance, while I am perishing here with hunger! I will go to my father and say, "Father, I have sinned and am no longer worthy to be called thy son. Make me one of thy hired men." '

5. "He arose and went to his father. But while he was yet a long way off, his father saw him and ran and kissed him. And the son said, 'Father I have sinned——'

6. "But the father called, 'Fetch the best robe and sandals! Kill the fattened calf. This my son was lost and is found!'

7. "His elder son, coming from the field, heard music and dancing, and inquired what this meant. They told him.

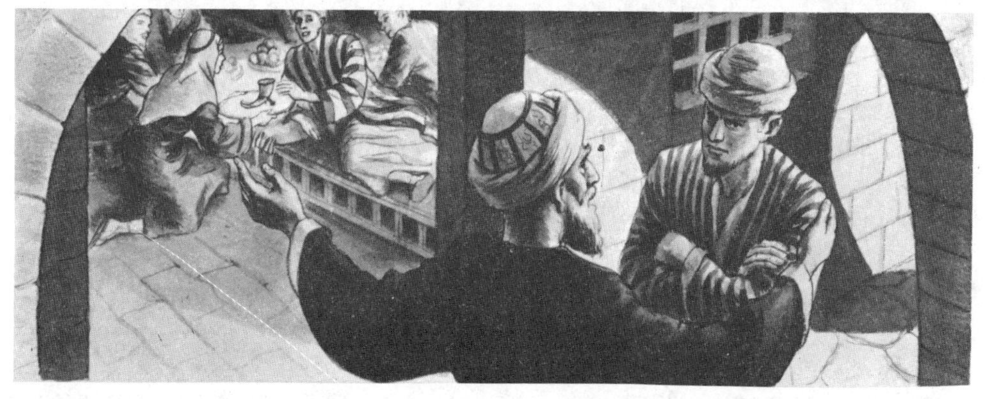

8. "He was angered and would not go in. His father came and begged him, but he answered, 'These many years I have been serving thee, and yet thou hast never given me a kid that I might make merry with my friends!' His father replied, 'Son, all that is mine is thine; but we were bound to rejoice, for this thy brother was lost and is found.' "

Rich man, beggar man

1. When the Pharisees sneered at Him, He said, "There was a rich man who used to clothe himself in purple and fine linen, and who feasted every day. A poor man named Lazarus lay at his gate, covered with sores, and longing to be filled with the crumbs that fell from the rich man's table. The poor man died and was borne away by the angels into Abraham's bosom; the rich man also died and was buried in hell.

2. "Lifting up his eyes in torment, he saw Abraham and Lazarus. And he cried out, 'Father Abraham, send Lazarus to comfort me!' But Abraham said, 'Son, between us a great gulf is fixed, that none can cross.' 'Then send him to my brothers. If someone from the dead goes to them, they will repent,' he pleaded. But Abraham answered, 'If they do not hearken to Moses and the Prophets, they will not believe—even if someone rises from the dead.' "

The raising of Lazarus

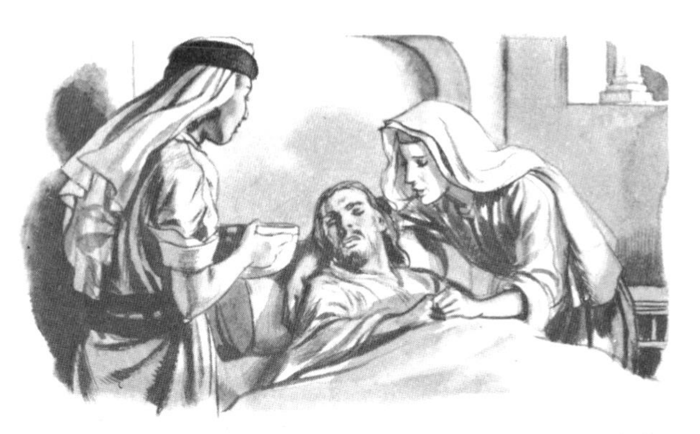

1. In Bethany lived another Lazarus, brother of Mary and Martha. Now Jesus loved the family, and when Lazarus was sick the sisters sent to Him.

2. But Jesus remained two more days where He was. Then He said, "Let us go into Judea." "Rabbi," the disciples answered, "the Jews were seeking to stone Thee there."

3. "Lazarus sleeps," He said to them. "I go that I may wake him." Thomas told his fellow-disciples, "Let us also go, that we may die with Him."

4. When Martha heard Jesus was coming, she came to meet Him, saying, "Lord, if Thou hadst been here, my brother would not have died." "Thy brother shall rise," Jesus answered. "I know he will rise on the last day," she replied. Jesus said, "I am the Resurrection and the Life; he who believes in Me shall never die."

5. Jesus came to the tomb. It was a cave, and a stone was laid against it.

6. "Take away the stone," Jesus said. Then, raising His eyes: "Father——

7. "—I give Thee thanks that Thou hast heard me. Yet I knew that Thou always hearest me." After this, He cried out with a loud voice, "Lazarus, come forth." And at once he who had been dead came forth. Many of the Jews who had seen what He did believed in Him. But some of them went away to the Pharisees, and told them.

8. The chief priests and the Pharisees gathered together a council. "If we let Him alone," they said, "all will believe in Him, and the Romans will come and take away both our place and our nation." But Caiphas said, "It is better for us that one man die for the people, instead of the whole nation perishing."

The ten lepers

1. As He was going to Jerusalem, there met Him ten lepers who stood afar off and lifted up their voices, crying:

2. "Jesus, Master, have pity on us." And when He saw them He said, "Go, show yourselves to the priests." And it came to pass, as they were on their way, that they were made clean.

3. One of them, seeing that he was made clean, returned and fell at His feet, giving thanks; he was a Samaritan. But Jesus said, "Were not ten made clean? Has no one been found to return and give glory to God except this foreigner?" And He said to him, "Arise, go thy way, for thy faith has saved thee."

The proud and the humble

1. He spoke this parable to some who considered themselves perfect and despised others. "Two men went to the Temple to pray, a Pharisee and a tax-collector. The Pharisee began to pray thus: 'God, I thank Thee that I am not like the rest of men.

2. " 'I fast twice a week, I pay tithes of all I possess.' But the tax-collector would not lift up his eyes, but kept striking his breast, saying:

3. " 'God, be merciful to me the sinner.' I tell you, this man went home justified rather than the other; for he who humbles himself shall be exalted."

The rich young ruler

1. As Jesus was going on His journey, a certain ruler asked Him, "Good Master, what shall I do to gain eternal life?" But Jesus said to him:

2. "Why dost thou call Me good? No one is good but God only. Thou knowest the commandments?"

3. The ruler said, "All these I have kept ever since I was a child." And Jesus, looking upon him, said:

4. "One thing is still lacking to thee: sell all that thou hast and give to the poor and thou shalt have treasures in heaven; and come, follow Me."

5. The ruler was grieved, for he was rich. Jesus, seeing him become sad, said, "With what difficulty will they who have riches enter the Kingdom of God!"

Jesus and the children

Little children were brought to Him that He might lay His hands on them and pray; but the disciples rebuked those who brought them. Jesus said, "Let the children come to Me, for of such is the Kingdom of God. Amen I say to you, whoever does not accept the Kingdom of God as a little child, will not enter into it." And He put His arms about them, and began to bless them.

The laborers in the vineyard

1. Jesus said, "The Kingdom of Heaven is like a householder who went out early to hire laborers for his vineyard.

2. "Having agreed for a denarius a day, he sent them into his vineyard. About the third, sixth, ninth, and eleventh hour he went out and found others and said:

3. " 'Go also to the vineyard.' When evening had come, they of the eleventh hour received each a denarius. The first in their turn also received a denarius.

4. "They began to murmur, 'These last have worked a single hour, and thou hast put them on a level with us.' Answering one, he said, 'Didst thou not agree for a denarius? I choose to give this last even as to thee.' Even so the last shall be first, and the first last; for many are called, but few are chosen."

How to be great

1. Going to Jerusalem, He took the twelve disciples aside and said, "The Son of Man will be betrayed, scourged and crucified; and on the third day He will rise again."

2. The mother of James and John came, and worshipping, said, "Command that these my sons may sit at Thy right and left, in Thy Kingdom."

3. Jesus asked the two brothers, "Can you drink the cup I am about to drink?" They said, "We can." He told them, "Of My cup you shall indeed drink——

4. "—but as for sitting at My right and left, that is not Mine to give." The other ten were indignant at the brothers. But Jesus said, "Whoever wishes to become great among you shall be your servant; even as the Son of Man has not come to be served but to serve, and to give His life as a ransom for many."

The story of Zacchaeus

1. He entered Jericho. There Zacchaeus, a leading tax-collector and rich, was trying to see Jesus, but could not on account of the crowd, because he was small of stature.

2. So he ran ahead and climbed a sycamore tree. Jesus looked up and said, "Zacchaeus, I must stay in thy house today."

3. Zacchaeus came down and welcomed Him joyfully. All began to murmur, "He has gone to be the guest of a sinner."

4. But Zacchaeus stood up and said to the Lord, "Behold, Lord, I give one-half of my possessions to the poor, and if I have defrauded anyone of anything, I restore it fourfold." Jesus said to him, "Today salvation has come to this house. For the Son of Man came to seek and to save what was lost."

The parable of the talents

1. "The Kingdom of Heaven," said Jesus, "is like a man going abroad, who called his servants and delivered to them his goods. To one he gave five talents, to another two, and to another one, and then departed.

2. "He who received the five talents traded with them, and gained five more. He who received the two gained two more.

3. "But he who received the one talent hid it. After a long time the master came and settled accounts with them.

4. "To the first two he said, 'Well done, good and faithful servants; because you have been faithful over a few things, I will set you over many.'

5. "But because the third had made no use of his talent the master said, 'Wicked and slothful servant! Cast him forth into the darkness outside.' "

Supper at Bethany

1. Jesus, six days before the Passover, came to Bethany, to the house of Lazarus, whom He had raised from the dead.

2. Lazarus and his sisters made Him a supper there, and Martha served. Mary took a pound of ointment of great value, and anointed the feet of Jesus, and with her hair wiped His feet dry. And the house was filled with the odor of the ointment. Then one of His disciples, Judas Iscariot, he who was about to betray Him, said:

3. "Why was this ointment not sold for three hundred denarii, and given to the poor?" Now he said this, not that he cared for the poor, but because he was a thief, and holding the purse, used to take what was put into it.

4. "Let her be," Jesus answered. "She has done Me a good turn. The poor you have always with you, but you do not always have Me."

Palm Sunday

1. The next day, Sunday, He drew near Jerusalem and came to Bethpage on the Mount of Olives. Jesus sent two disciples, saying, "Go into the village opposite you, and you will find a colt tied. Bring it to Me. And if anyone say anything, you shall say that the Lord has need of it, and immediately he will send it."

4. The crowd took the branches of palms and went forth to meet Him. Many spread their cloaks upon the road. The whole company of disciples began to rejoice, saying, "Blessed is He Who comes as King in the name of the Lord! Peace in Heaven, and glory in the Highest!" And He went into Jerusalem.

2. They found the colt tied at a door and loosed it. Some bystanders said, "Why are you loosing the colt?" But they answered as Jesus told them to——

3. —and the bystanders let them go. They brought the colt to Jesus, and threw their cloaks over it, and He sat upon it. Those who went before Him cried, "Hosanna!"

5. Some of the Pharisees from the crowds said, "Master, rebuke Thy disciples." But He answered, "I tell you that if these keep silence the stones will cry out."

Cleansing the Temple

1. Entering the Temple, Jesus found men selling oxen, sheep and doves, and money-changers at tables. By law the Jews were allowed to sell animals to the worshippers for sacrifice, but the House of the Lord had become a house of business where men were cheated.

2. Making a whip of cords, He drove them all out of the Temple, also the sheep and oxen, and He poured out the money of the changers and overturned the tables, and the seats of those who sold the doves. And He said to them, "It is written, 'My house shall be called a house of prayer,' but you have made it a den of thieves."

3. The Jews asked, "What sign of authority dost Thou show, seeing that Thou dost these things?" In answer Jesus said:

4. "Destroy this temple, and in three days I will raise it up." But He was speaking of the temple of His body.

"By what authority?"

1. Next morning, in the Temple, the elders came as He was teaching, and said again, "By what authority dost Thou do these things?" But Jesus answered, "By what authority did John baptize?" Now they could not agree that it was God's, since they did not believe in John.

2. Nor dared they say it was man's, since the people held John to be a prophet. So they answered, "We do not know." "Neither do I tell you My authority," He replied.

3. Jesus said, "A man asked his two sons to work in his vineyard. The first refused, but later repented and went. The second said, 'I go,' but did not.

4. "Which of the two did the father's will?" Jesus asked. They said, "The first." "Amen," said Jesus. "The tax-collectors and sinners are entering the Kingdom of God before you. For they believed John but you did not, nor did you repent afterwards."

The royal wedding feast

1. Jesus spoke to them again in parables, saying, "The Kingdom of Heaven is like a king who made a marriage feast for his son. And he sent his servants to call in those invited to the marriage feast, but they would not come.

2. "They made light of it, and went off, one to his farm——

3. "—and another to his business; and the rest laid hold of his servants.

4. "They treated them shamefully, and killed them. The king heard of it.

5. "He was angry, and he sent armies and destroyed those murderers, and burnt their city. Then he said to his servants, 'The marriage feast indeed is ready, but those who were invited were not worthy.

6. " 'Go therefore to the crossroads and invite to the marriage feast whomever you shall find.' And his servants went out into the roads, and gathered all whom they found, both good and bad; and the marriage feast was filled with guests."

The wicked tenants

1. Jesus said, "A householder planted a vineyard and put a hedge about it. Then he let it out to vine-dressers.

2. "When the fruit season drew near, he sent servants to receive some of the fruit as rent. The vine-dressers beat one and killed another, and stoned another.

3. "Finally he sent his son, saying, 'They will respect my son.' But the vine-dressers said, 'Let us kill him and have his inheritance.' So they killed him.

4. "When the owner of the vineyard comes," Jesus asked, "what will he do to those vine-dressers?" The priests answered, "Destroy those evil men and let the vineyard to other vine-dressers." Jesus replied, "Therefore I say to you that the Kingdom of God will be taken away from you and will be given to a people yielding its fruits."

Tribute to Caesar

1. The chief priests, watching their opportunity, sent forth spies, that they might entrap Him in His talk and deliver Him up to the ruling power. And they asked Him, "Master, we know that Thou showest no favor to any but teachest the way of God in truth. Is it lawful for us to give tribute to Caesar or not?" He saw their craftiness.

2. If He said yes, they would denounce Him to the people; if He said no, they would denounce Him to the Romans. So He replied, "Show Me a denarius. Whose image and inscription does it bear?" They said, "Caesar's." And He answered, "Render, therefore, to Caesar the things that are Caesar's, and to God the things that are God's."

“The greatest commandment”

1. The Pharisees gathered together. One of them, a doctor of the Holy Law, putting Him to the test, asked Him, “Master, which is the great commandment in the Law?”

2. Jesus said to him, “ ‘Thou shalt love the Lord thy God with thy whole heart, and with thy whole soul, and with thy whole mind.’

3. “This is the greatest and the first commandment. The second is like it: ‘Thou shalt love thy neighbor as thyself.’ On these commandments depends the whole Law.”

4. And the Scribe replied, “Well answered, Master, Thou hast said truly that these things are greater than all burnt offerings and sacrifices.” Jesus, seeing that the man had answered wisely, said to him, “Thou art not far from the Kingdom of God.”

The widow's mite

1. Teaching in the Temple, He said to His disciples, "Beware of the Scribes who like to walk about in long robes, and love greetings in the market place, and front seats in the synagogue; who devour the houses of the widows, making pretense of long prayers." Jesus sat down opposite the Temple treasury. He saw the rich putting in their gifts.

2. And He saw also a certain poor widow putting in two mites. And He said, "Truly, this poor widow has put in more than all. For they have put in out of their abundance; but she has put in all that she had to live on."

"I will draw all men unto Me"

1. Certain Gentiles approached Philip, saying, "Sir, we wish to see Jesus." Philip and Andrew spoke to Jesus, but He answered them, "The hour has come——

2. "—for the Son of Man to be glorified. Unless the grain of wheat falls into the ground and dies, it remains alone. But if it dies, it brings forth much fruit.

3. "Father, glorify Thy name!" There came a voice from heaven: "I have, and will again." The crowd said it had thundered. Others said, "An angel has spoken to Him."

4. Jesus went on, "Now will the Prince of the world be cast out. And I, if I be lifted up from the earth, will draw all men unto Me." He knew how he was to die.

Destruction of the Temple

1. As Jesus left the Temple, some said that it was adorned with beautiful stones.

2. Jesus answered, "The days will come in which there will not be left one stone upon another." Later, as He was sitting on the Mount of Olives, the disciples came to Him, saying, "When are these things to happen, and what will be the sign of Thy coming and of the end of the world?" In answer Jesus said:

3. "You shall hear of wars and rumors of wars. These things must come to pass, but the end is not yet. For nation will rise against nation, and kingdom against kingdom.

4. "There will be pestilences and famines and earthquakes in various places, terrors and great signs from heaven. But all these things are the beginnings of sorrow.

5. "Many will fall away, and will betray one another. And many false prophets will arise, and will lead many astray.

6. "But whoever perseveres shall be saved. And this gospel of the Kingdom shall be preached in the whole world.

7. "Be on your guard," Jesus went on, "for they will deliver you up to councils, and you will be beaten in synagogues, and you will stand before governors and kings for My sake. I Myself will give you wisdom, which all your adversaries will not be able to gainsay. But some of you they will put to death.

8. "And when you see Jerusalem surrounded by an army, then know that her desolation is at hand. Then let those who are in Judea flee to the mountains, and let those who are in the country not enter her. For these are the days of vengeance."

The wise and foolish maidens

1. "You must be ready for the Kingdom of Heaven," Jesus said, and He told a story about ten bridesmaids who were to meet a bridegroom at night. As he was long in coming, they all became drowsy and slept.

2. Five were wise and carried spare oil for their lamps, but five were foolish and did not. When he came, the lamps of the foolish were going out.

3. They asked the wise for oil but were told, "There may not be enough; go and buy for yourselves." Those who were ready went to the marriage feast.

4. The door was shut. Finally the foolish bridesmaids came back and cried, "Open the door!" But the bridegroom answered:

5. "I do not know you." Jesus added, "Watch, for you know neither the day nor hour when the Son of Man is coming."

The Last

1. "When the Son of Man shall come in His majesty, and all the angels with Him, then He will sit on the throne of His glory. Before Him will be gathered all the nations,

2. "Then the King will say to those on His right hand, 'Come, blessed of My Father, take possession of the Kingdom prepared for you from the foundation of the world. For I was hungry and you gave Me to eat; I was thirsty and you gave Me to drink; I was a stranger and you took Me in; naked, and you covered me; sick, and you visited Me; in prison, and you came to Me.' Then the just will answer, 'Lord, when did we see Thee hungry or thirsty, a stranger, or naked, or sick, or in prison?' And the King will say, 'As long as you did it for the least of My brethren, you did it for Me.'

Judgment

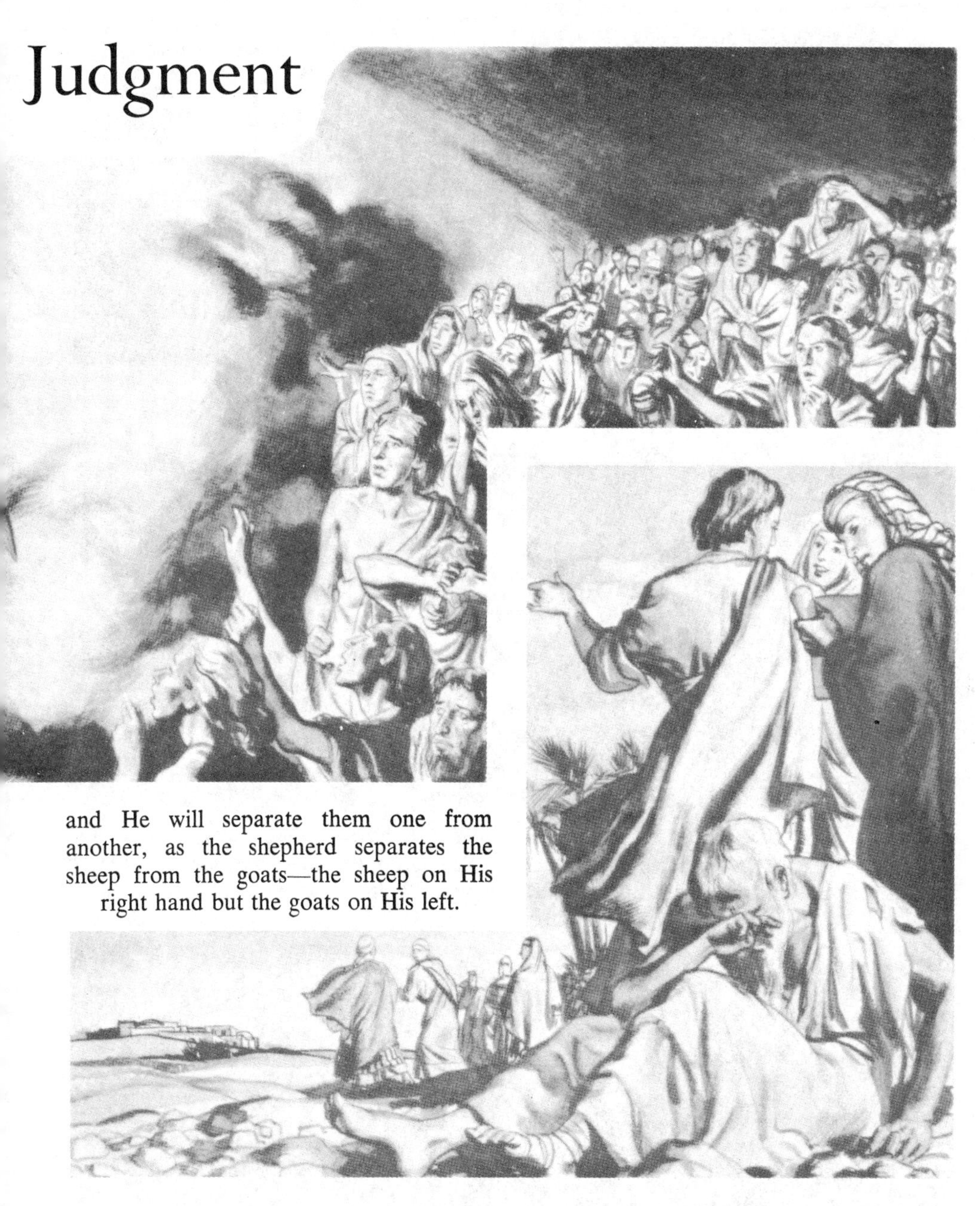

and He will separate them one from another, as the shepherd separates the sheep from the goats—the sheep on His right hand but the goats on His left.

3. "Then He will say to those on His left hand, 'Depart from Me, accursed ones, into the everlasting fire which was prepared for the devil and his angels. For I was hungry, and you did not give Me to eat; I was thirsty and you gave Me no drink; I was a stranger and you did not take Me in; naked, and you did not clothe Me; sick, and in prison, and you did not visit Me.' Then they also will answer, 'Lord, when did we see Thee hungry, or thirsty, or a stranger, or naked, or sick, or in prison?' Then He will say, 'As long as you did not do it for one of these least ones, you did not do it for Me.' "

Judas sells his soul

1. When Jesus had finished these words, He said to His disciples, "After two days the Passover will be here, and the Son of Man will be delivered up to be crucified."

2. The chief priests and the elders of the people gathered together in the court of the high priest, who was called Caiphas, and they took counsel together how they might seize Jesus by stealth and put Him to death. But they said, "Not on the feast, or there might be a riot among the people."

3. One of the Twelve, Judas Iscariot, went to them and said, "What will you give me if I deliver Him to you?"

4. They counted him out thirty pieces of silver. From then on he was watching for an opportunity to betray Him.

The Last Supper

1. On Thursday, the day before the Passover, He sent Peter and John into the city, saying, "Meet a man carrying a pitcher of water; follow him into his house and say, 'The Master asks: Where is the guest chamber, where I may eat the Passover with My disciples?'

2. "He will show you a large upper room; there make ready." They went and found just as He had told them. When evening arrived, He reclined at table with the Twelve.

3. There arose a dispute among them, which of them was the greatest. He rose from the supper, poured water into the basin and began to wash the disciples' feet.

4. He came to Peter. Peter said to Him, "Thou shalt never wash my feet!" "If I do not wash thee, thou shalt have no part with Me," Jesus answered. Then Peter said to Him, "Lord, not my feet only, but also my hands and head."

1. After He had washed their feet, He said, "You call Me Master and Lord, and I have washed your feet. I have given you an example that as I have done to you, you also should do. No servant is greater than his master." When Jesus had said these things, He

2. One of His disciples, John, whom Jesus loved, was reclining at Jesus' bosom. Peter said to him, "Who is it of whom He speaks?"

3. John, leaning back upon the bosom of Jesus, said to Him, "Lord, who is it?" Jesus answered, "It is he for whom I shall dip the bread——"

was troubled in spirit, and told them solemnly, "One of you will betray Me—one who is eating with Me. The hand of him who betrays Me is on this table." The disciples looked at one another. Being very much saddened, they began each to say, "Is it I, Lord?"

4. "—and give it to him." And when He had dipped the bread, He gave it to Judas Iscariot and said to him, "What thou dost, do quickly."

5. None at the table understood why He said this. When Judas had received the morsel, he went out quickly. And it was night.

The Lord's Supper

1. While they were at supper, Jesus took the bread and the wine, and He gave thanks and blessed them.

2. He broke the bread and gave it to His disciples. "Take and eat," He said. "This is My body, which is being given for you. Do this in remembrance of Me."

3. He took also the cup and gave it to them, saying, "Drink of this; this is My blood, which is being shed for many unto the forgiveness of sins.

4. "This cup is the new covenant. I will not drink henceforth of this fruit of the vine, until that day when I shall drink it new with you in the Kingdom of My Father. As often as you eat this bread and drink the cup, you proclaim the death of the Lord until He comes." And after reciting a hymn, they went out to the Mount of Olives.

Peter's confidence

1. As they went their way, Jesus said, "I shall be with you only a little while. A new commandment I give you, that you love one another as I have loved you.

2. "By this will all men know you are My disciples. Let not your heart be troubled. You believe in God, believe also in Me. I go to prepare a place for you. And if I go, I am coming again, and I will take you to Myself, that where I am, there you also may be. And where I go you know, and the way you know."

3. Peter said to Him, "Lord, where art Thou going?" Jesus answered, "Where I am going thou canst not follow Me now, but thou shalt follow later.

4. "I say to thee, this very night, before a cock crows, thou wilt deny Me three times." "Even if I should die, I will not deny Thee!" Peter cried.

5. Thomas said to Him, "Lord, we do not know where Thou art going, and how can we know the way?"

6. Jesus said to him, "I am the Way, the Truth, and the Life. No one comes to the Father but through Me."

7. Philip said, "Lord, show us the Father." "Have I been so long with you, and you have not known Me? Philip, he who sees Me sees also the Father.

8. "I am the Vine, and My Father is the Vine-dresser. Every branch in Me that bears no fruit He will take away; and every branch that bears fruit——

9. "—He will cleanse, that it may bear more fruit. Abide in Me, and I in you. I am the Vine, you are the branches. He who abides in Me, and I in him, he bears much fruit, for without Me you can do nothing. Greater love than this no one has, that one lay down his life for his friends."

Gethsemani

1. He came to the Mount of Olives, to a garden called Gethsemani, and the disciples followed Him. And He said to His disciples, "Sit down here while I go over yonder and pray." He took with Him Peter and James and John.

2. Jesus began to feel dread and to be exceedingly troubled. And He said to them, "My soul is sad, even unto death. Wait here and watch." And going forward a little, He fell on the ground, and began to pray, saying, "Father, all things are possible to Thee. If Thou art willing——

3. "—remove this cup from Me; yet not My will but Thine be done." And there appeared to Him an angel from heaven to strengthen Him.

4. Falling into an agony, He prayed more earnestly. His sweat became as drops of blood running down upon the ground. Then He arose from prayer.

5. He came to the three disciples and found them sleeping. And He said to Peter, "Dost thou sleep? Couldst thou not watch one hour? Watch and pray, that you may not enter into temptation. The spirit indeed is willing, but the flesh is weak."

6. Again He went away and prayed. And He came again and found them sleeping, for their eyes were heavy. They did not know what answer to make to Him. He came the third time, and said, "The hour has come. Behold, he who will betray Me is at hand!" While He was speaking, Judas came with a great crowd.

7. The betrayer had arranged with the officers a signal, saying, "Whomever I kiss, that is He; lay hold of Him."

8. He went straight to Jesus and kissed Him. But Jesus said, "Judas, dost thou betray the Son of Man with a kiss?"

9. They came forward and set hands on Jesus. Peter, having a sword, drew it and struck the servant of the high priest and cut off his ear.

10. "Put up thy sword!" Jesus cried. "Shall I not drink the cup that the Father has given me?" And He healed the servant's ear.

11. But Jesus said to the chief priests and captains of the Temple, "As against a robber have you come out, with swords and clubs. When I was daily with you in the Temple, you did not stretch forth your hands against Me." Now all this was done that the Scriptures might be fulfilled. Then all His disciples left Him and fled.

The trial of Jesus

1. The cohort and the tribune and the attendants of the Jews bound Him. And they brought Him to Annas, father-in-law of Caiphas, the high priest. Annas questioned Jesus concerning His disciples, and His teachings. Jesus answered him, "Why dost thou question Me?

2. "I have spoken openly to the world. Question those who have heard what I spoke." When He had said these things, one of the attendants struck Jesus.

3. "Is that the way Thou dost answer?" he cried. Jesus answered, "If I have spoken ill, bear witness to the evil; but if well, why dost thou strike Me?"

4. Annas sent Him bound to Caiphas. Peter followed, even to the courtyard of the high priest. One of the maidservants looked at him and said:

5. "Thou wast with Jesus of Nazareth." But he denied it, saying, "I neither know nor understand what thou art saying." And he went outside into the vestibule.

6. Now the chief priests and all the Sanhedrin were seeking witness against Jesus, that they might put Him to death, but they found none. For while many bore false witness against Him, their evidence did not agree.

7. Jesus kept silence. The high priest began to ask Him, "Art Thou the Christ, the Son of the Blessed One?" And Jesus said to him, "I am.

8. "And you shall see the Son of Man sitting at the right hand of the Power, coming with the clouds of heaven." The high priest tore his garments and said:

9. "What further need have we of witnesses? You have heard the blasphemy." And they all condemned Him as liable to death. Some began to spit on Him.

10. While Peter was below, the maidservant, seeing him again, began to say to the bystanders, "This is one of them." But again he denied it.

11. After a little while the bystanders again said to Peter, "Surely thou art one of them, for thou art also a Galilean." But he began to swear: "I do not know this Man you are talking about."

12. The men who had Him in custody began to mock Him and beat Him. And they blindfolded Him, and kept striking His face and asking Him, "Prophesy, who is it that struck Thee?" And many other things they kept saying against Him, reviling Him.

13. They led Jesus to the praetorium, the fortress of the Roman governor. A cock crowed. The Lord turned and looked upon Peter. And Peter remembered the word of the Lord, how He said:

14. "Before a cock crows, thou wilt deny Me three times." Peter went out and wept bitterly.

The end of Judas

1. Judas, who betrayed Him, repented when he saw that He was condemned. He brought back the thirty pieces of silver——

2. —to the chief priests and the elders, saying, "I have sinned in betraying innocent blood." But they said:

3. "What is that to us? See to it thyself." He flung the pieces of silver into the Temple and withdrew.

4. Judas went away and hanged himself. The chief priests took the pieces of silver and said, "It is not lawful to put them into the treasury——

5. "—seeing that it is the price of blood." And after they consulted together, they bought with them the potter's field, as a burial place for strangers.

Sentence of death

1. The chief priests delivered Him to Pilate, the Roman governor. And they began to accuse Him, saying, "We have found this Man saying that He is Christ, a King. He is stirring up the people throughout all Judea, beginning from Galilee to this place."

2. Pilate sent Him to Herod. When Herod saw Jesus, he was glad, because he had heard much about Him, and was hoping to see some miracles done by Him.

3. He put many questions to Him, but as He made no answer, Herod sent Him back to Pilate. Pilate asked Him, "Art Thou the King of the Jews?"

4. Jesus answered, "I am a King, but My Kingdom is not of this world. I have come to bear witness to the Truth."

5. "What is Truth?" Pilate said. And when Jesus was accused by the chief priests, He still made no answer.

6. Now Pilate's wife sent a message: "Have nothing to do with that just Man; I suffered much in a dream about Him."

7. So Pilate went outside to the Jews and said to them, "I find no guilt in Him. But you have a custom that I should release someone to you at the Passover. Do you wish that I release to you the King of the Jews?" "Not this Man, but Barabbas," they all cried out. Now Barabbas was a robber.

8. Pilate took Jesus and had Him scourged. And the soldiers, plaiting a crown of thorns, put it upon His head, and arrayed Him in a purple cloak. And they kept coming to Him and saying, "Hail, King of the Jews!" and striking Him.

9. Jesus was brought forth, wearing the crown of thorns and the purple cloak. Pilate said to the crowd, "Behold the Man!" And they cried out, "Crucify Him!" "Take Him yourselves and crucify Him, for I find no guilt in Him," Pilate said to them.

10. The Jews answered, "We have a Law, and according to that Law He must die, because He has made Himself out to be the Son of God." Now Pilate was afraid.

11. Again he examined Jesus. "Where art Thou from? Speak—dost Thou not know I can crucify Thee?" Jesus answered, "Thou wouldst have no power over Me—

12. "—were it not given thee from above." Once more Pilate looked for a way to release Him. But the Jews cried out, saying, "If thou release this Man, thou art no friend of Caesar; for everyone who makes himself king sets himself against Caesar."

13. Pilate, when he heard these words, brought Jesus outside. And he said to the Jews, "Behold, your King!" But they cried out, "Away with Him! Crucify Him!" "Shall I crucify your King?" Pilate said to them. The chief priests answered, "We have no King but Caesar."

14. Pilate, seeing a riot was breaking out, washed his hands in sight of the crowd, saying, "I am innocent of the blood of this just Man."

15. All the people answered, "His blood be on us and on our children." Then Pilate pronounced sentence, and handed Him over to be crucified.

The Crucifixion

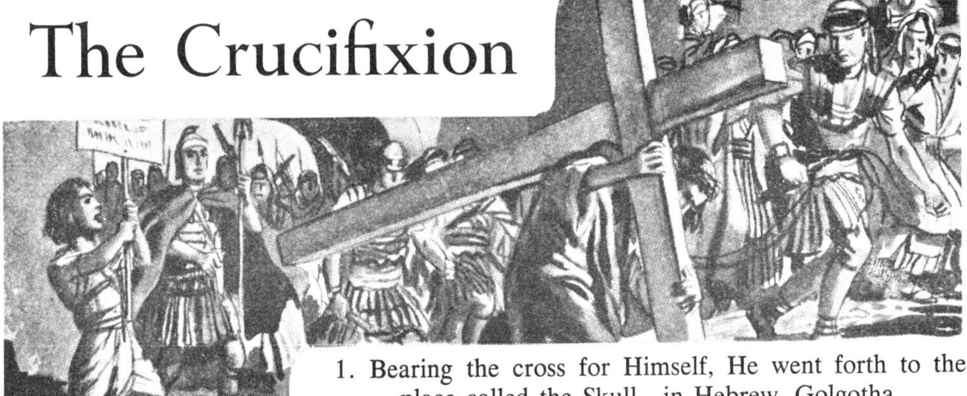

1. Bearing the cross for Himself, He went forth to the place called the Skull—in Hebrew, Golgotha.

2. As they went, the soldiers laid hold of a certain Simon of Cyrene, coming from the country, and upon him they laid the cross, to bear it after Jesus.

3. There was following Him a great crowd of women, lamenting Him. Jesus, turning, said, "Do not weep for Me, but weep for yourselves and for your children.

4. "For days are coming in which men will say to the mountains, 'Fall upon us,' and to the hills, 'Cover us!' " At last they came to Golgotha, the Place of the Skull. The soldiers gave Him wine to drink, mixed with myrrh, but He did not take it.

5. Now they crucified Him, and two robbers with Him, one on His right hand and one on His left. Jesus said, "Father, forgive them, for they do not know what they are doing." And they put above His head the charge against Him: "Jesus, the King of the Jews."

6. Many read this inscription. The chief priests said, therefore, to Pilate, "Do not write 'The King of the Jews'——

7. "—but, 'He *said*, I am the King of the Jews.' " "What I have written, I have written," Pilate answered.

8. The soldiers took His garments and made of them four parts, to each soldier a part. The tunic they cast lots for. And sitting down, they kept watch over Him.

9. The passers-by were jeering, "If Thou art the Son of God, come down from the cross!" The priests said in mockery, "He saved others, Himself He cannot save!"

10. One of the robbers was abusing Him, saying, "If Thou art the Christ, save Thyself and us." But the other rebuked him: "We are receiving what our deeds deserved; but this Man has done nothing wrong." And, to Jesus: "Lord, remember me when Thou comest into Thy Kingdom." "This day," Jesus said to him, "thou shalt be with Me in Paradise."

11. Jesus saw His mother and the disciple John standing by. "Woman," He said to His mother, "behold thy son." Then He said to the disciple, "Behold thy mother." And from that hour the disciple took her into his home.

12. The sun was darkened, and Jesus cried out with a loud voice, "My God, My God, why hast Thou forsaken Me?" Some of the bystanders said:

13. "He is calling Elias." After this Jesus said, "I thirst!" Someone soaked a sponge in wine, put it on a reed and offered it to Him.

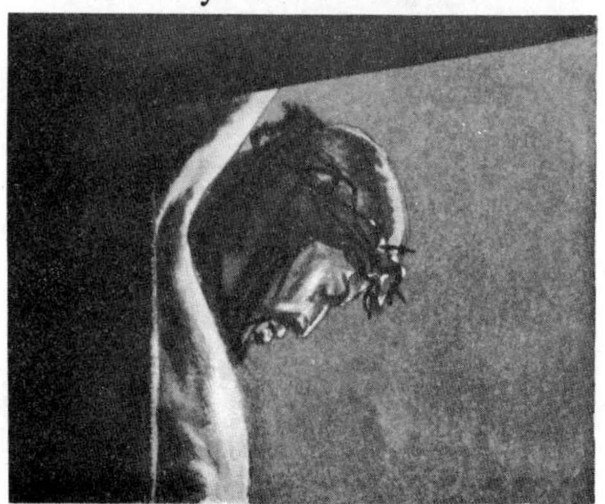

14. There was darkness over the land for three hours. Then Jesus cried out, " It is consummated! Father, into Thy hands I commend My spirit!" And He expired.

15. When the centurion, who stood facing Him, saw how He had cried out and expired, he said, "Truly this Man was the Son of God!"

The Resurrection

1. A disciple of Jesus, Joseph of Arimathea, a councillor of high rank, went in boldly to Pilate and asked for the body of Jesus. Pilate, when he learned that one of the soldiers had opened His side with a lance to ensure death, granted the body.

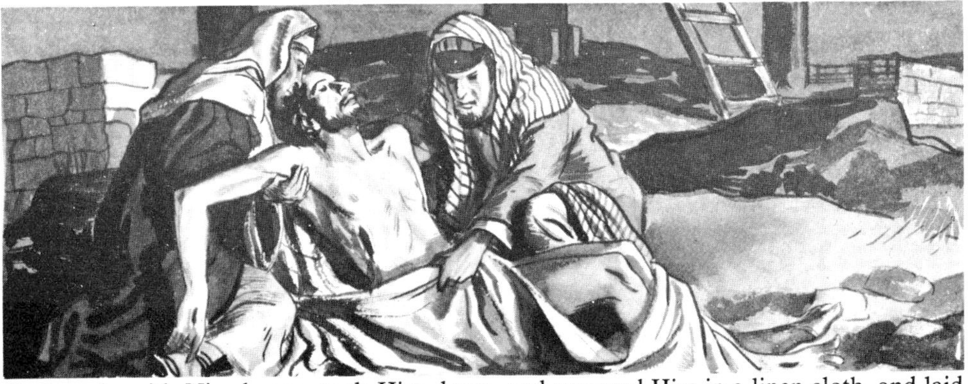

2. Joseph, with Nicodemus, took Him down, and wrapped Him in a linen cloth, and laid Him in a rock-hewn tomb, where no one had yet been laid, in a garden. Mary Magdalene, Mary the mother of James, and Salome—the women who had come with Him from Galilee—were looking on.

3. Joseph and Nicodemus rolled a large stone to the entrance of the tomb. As the Sabbath was drawing on, the women went back and prepared spices and ointments.

4. The chief priests remembered that Jesus had said, "After three days I will rise again." So they made the sepulchre secure, and set a guard over it.

5. On the first day of the week, the women came to the tomb, when the sun had just risen. They were saying, "Who will roll the stone back from the entrance of the tomb for us?" And looking up, they saw that the stone had been rolled back.

6. On entering, they did not find the body of the Lord Jesus. But they saw a young man sitting, in a white robe. He said, "Why do you seek the living one among the dead? He has risen, He is not here. But go, tell His disciples that He goes before you into Galilee; there you shall see Him, as He told you."

7. They departed quickly from the tomb in fear and great joy. Mary Magdalene ran to Peter and John and said to them, "They have taken the Lord from the tomb, and we do not know where they have laid Him." Peter and John went to the tomb, running, and saw the linen clothes lying there. Wondering, the disciples went away.

8. Mary was standing outside, weeping at the tomb. She turned round and beheld Jesus, and did not know it was He. Jesus said, "Woman, why art thou weeping?"

9. She, thinking He was the gardener, said to Him, "Sir, if thou hast removed Him, tell me where thou hast laid Him and I will take Him away."

10. Jesus said to her, "Mary!" "Master!" she cried. "Do not cling to Me," Jesus said, "for I have not yet ascended to My Father, but go——

11. "—to My brethren and say to them, I ascend to My Father and your Father, to My God and your God." And Jesus also met others and spoke to them.

The soldiers bribed

1. Some of the guard reported to the chief priests all that had happened in the night at the tomb.

2. There had been a great earthquake, they said. An angel of the Lord came down from heaven and, drawing near, rolled back the stone and sat upon it.

3. His countenance was like lightning, and his raiment like snow. And for fear of him the guards were terrified, and became like dead men.

4. The chief priests assembled with the elders and consulted together. They gave much money to the soldiers, telling them, "Say, 'His disciples came by night and stole Him while we were sleeping.' And if the governor hears of this, we will persuade him and keep you out of trouble." The soldiers took the money, and did as they were instructed.

The Emmaus road

1. Two of the disciples were going that very day to a village named Emmaus. While they were conversing, Jesus Himself drew near and went along with them, but they did not recognize Him. He said, "What words are you exchanging as you walk and are sad?"

2. One of them, Cleophas, answered, "Art thou the only stranger in Jerusalem who does not know that Jesus of Nazareth, a prophet mighty before God and the people——

3. "—was delivered up and crucified? Certain women of our company did not find His body at the tomb and say that angels told them He is alive." Jesus answered:

4. "Did not the Christ have to suffer before entering into glory?" And He interpreted the Scriptures referring to Himself. At the village, He went in with them.

5. At table with them, He took the bread, blessed it and broke it and began handing it to them. Suddenly they recognized Him; but He vanished from their sight.

"The Lord has risen"

1. They said, "Was not our heart burning within us while He was speaking?" Rising up that very hour, they returned to Jerusalem, where they found the apostles gathered together, and those who were with them, saying, "The Lord has risen indeed, and has appeared to Peter!"

2. The two began to relate what had happened on the journey, and how they recognized Him in the breaking of the bread. While they were talking, Jesus stood in their midst, and said, "Peace to you!" They were startled, and thought they saw a spirit. But He said to them, "Feel Me and see—a spirit does not have flesh and bones!"

3. The disciples rejoiced at the sight of the Lord. And He breathed upon them, and said, "Receive the Holy Spirit. Whose sins you shall forgive, they are forgiven; whose sins you shall retain, they are retained."

4. Thomas was not with them when Jesus came. When the other disciples told him, "We have seen the Lord," he replied:

5. "Unless I see in His hands the print of the nails, and put my hand into His side, I will not believe."

6. After eight days, Jesus came again to His disciples. He said to Thomas, "Bring here thy finger, and see My hands—put thy hand into My side; and be not unbelieving, but believing!" Thomas answered, "My Lord and my God!" "Because thou hast seen Me thou has believed," Jesus said. "Blessed are they who have not seen, and yet have believed."

Peter and the risen Lord

1. After this, the disciples went into Galilee. At Tiberias, Peter said, "I am going fishing." They answered, "We are going with thee." That night they caught nothing. When day was breaking, Jesus stood on the beach, yet they did not know Him.

2. Jesus called, "Young men, have you any fish?" They answered, "No." "Cast the net to the right of the boat," He said.

3. They cast, and caught a great number of fishes. John said, "It is the Lord!" Peter girt his tunic about him——

4. —and threw himself into the sea. The others came with the boat. They saw a fire, a fish upon it, and bread. Jesus said, "Bring some of the fishes."

5. Peter hauled the net onto the land. Then Jesus said, "Come and breakfast." No one dared to ask, "Who art Thou?", knowing that it was the Lord.

6. When they had breakfasted, Jesus said to Peter, "Dost thou love Me more than these do?" "Yes, Lord, Thou knowest that I love Thee," Peter said. Jesus answered, "Feed My lambs." Then Jesus asked a second time, "Dost thou love Me?"

7. "Lord, Thou *knowest* that I love Thee!" "Feed my lambs." A third time He asked, "Dost thou love Me?" Peter was grieved and said, "Lord, Thou knowest all——

8. "—Thou knowest that I love Thee." "Feed My sheep," Jesus said again; then: "When thou art old, another will lead thee where thou wouldst not."

9. Turning round, Peter saw John following them, and said to Jesus, "Lord, and what of this man?" Jesus answered him, "If I wish him to remain until I come, what is it to thee? Do thou follow Me."

He appears to many

1. The eleven disciples went to a mountain in Galilee where Jesus had directed them to go. When they, with more than five hundred of His followers, saw Him, they worshipped Him; but some doubted. Then Jesus drew near and said, "All power in heaven and on earth has been given to Me. Go, therefore, and make disciples of all nations.

2. "Baptize them in the name of the Father, and of the Son, and of the Holy Spirit, teaching them to observe all that I have commanded you; and behold, I am with you all days, even unto the end of the world."

The Ascension

1. Jesus showed Himself alive after His Passion by many proofs, during forty days appearing and speaking of the Kingdom of God.

2. Then He led the disciples out towards Bethany; and there, on the Mount of Olives, He blessed them.

3. And it came to pass, as He blessed them, that He parted from them and was carried up into heaven.

4. While they were gazing up, two men stood by them in white garments, and said, "Men of Galilee, why do you stand looking up to heaven? Jesus, Who has been taken up from you, shall come in the same way as you have seen Him going up to heaven."

PART II

The Story of His People

JESUS was born among the Jews, in Palestine, nearly two thousand years ago. To understand why, one must know their history. In this section are the stories of His people as His mother must have told them to Him, and the truths His teachers taught, selected from the history of the Jews as we have it in our Old Testament. The section ends with a brief account of their history in the years between the rebuilding of the Temple and the birth of our Lord. We have not attempted to separate stories which some scholars regard as mere tales told to stress a truth, from stories of actual happenings. Here, then, are the stories Jesus loved—of His people and God's dealings with them, and their hopes of a Deliverer ("Messias" or "Savior") which He knew Himself to be fulfilling.

Beginning with the Hebrew account of the Creation and man's disobedience, we shall see how God worked through the centuries to bring man back to Himself. First He chose a man, Abraham, with whom He made a "covenant" —called the Old Covenant (so our "Old Testament") to distinguish it from the New Covenant (so our "New Testament"), which He made with Jesus. Through Abraham God raised up a family—Jacob, whom He called Israel, and his twelve sons, the fathers of the twelve tribes of Israel. Then He shaped them into a nation, giving them, through Moses, His Law summarized in the Ten Commandments, and bringing them to Palestine, the land He had promised to their forefathers. We shall see how He sent leaders and kings, priests and prophets to guide them, and how again and again they turned from Him and their story became full of defeat and pain and sorrow. Yet God never failed to love them and to purpose that through them the whole of mankind might know and serve Him until the Kingdom of God was in all men's hearts—"on earth as it is in heaven."

The story of

In the beginning God created the heavens and the earth. The earth was waste and void; darkness covered the abyss. God said, "Let there be light!" And there was light. God separated the light from the darkness, calling the light Day, the darkness Night. And there was evening and morning—the first day. The second day, God made a firmament and called it Heaven. Then, on the third day, God said, "Let the dry land appear!"

On the fifth day, God created the great sea monsters, all kinds of swimming creatures, and all birds. And God blessed them, saying, "Be fruitful, multiply." On the sixth day, God made all kinds of wild beasts, every kind of cattle and creature crawling on the ground. And God said, "Let us make mankind in Our image and likeness, and let them

the Creation

And so it was. God called the dry land Earth, and the waters Seas. Then God said, "Let the earth bring forth seed-bearing plants and all kinds of fruit trees." On the fourth day, God made the two great lights—the greater light to rule the day and the smaller one to rule the night—and He made the stars. God set them in the heavens to shed light upon the earth, to rule the day and the night and to separate the light from the darkness.

have dominion over every creature on the earth." And God created man in His image; male and female He created them. And God saw that all He had made was very good. On the sixth day, God finished the work He had been doing. And God blessed the seventh day and made it holy because on it He rested from all His work of creation.

The Garden of Eden

1. God formed man of the dust of the ground, breathed into his nostrils the breath of life, and man became a living being.

2. God had placed a garden in Eden, and He put there the man, who was called Adam. While he slept, God took one of his ribs and made it into a woman.

3. The man said, "She now is bone of my bone, and flesh of my flesh. She shall be called Woman." He named the woman Eve, and she became his wife.

4. God commanded the man, "Of every tree of the garden thou shalt eat, but not of the tree of knowledge of good and evil. If thou shalt eat of it, thou shalt die."

5. But the serpent said to the woman, "When you eat, you will be like God——

6. "—knowing good and evil." She took the fruit and gave some to her husband.

7. After they ate it, their eyes were opened, and they knew shame and fear. When they heard God, they hid themselves among the trees. God put a curse upon the serpent and said, "I will put enmity between thee and the woman, between thy seed and her seed; He shall crush thy head." To the woman He said:

8. "In pain shalt thou bring forth children." To Adam He said, "In the sweat of thy brow shalt thou eat bread till thou return to the earth, out of which thou wast taken; for dust thou art, and into dust thou shalt return." And God put them out of the garden and placed the cherubim and the flaming sword to guard the way to the tree of life.

Cain and Abel

1. Adam and Eve had two sons: Abel, a shepherd, and Cain, a farmer.

2. One day Cain brought the Lord an offering of fruit, and Abel brought some of his flock. The Lord was pleased with Abel, but for Cain he had no regard.

3. Cain was very angry and turned against Abel and slew him. Then the Lord said, "Where is thy brother Abel?" "Am I my brother's keeper?" Cain answered.

4. The Lord told him he would be an outcast because of his crime. "But everyone will try to kill me!" Cain cried.

5. But the Lord said, "Not so! Whoever shall kill Cain shall be punished." Then He gave Cain a token so that no one should kill him. And Cain went and dwelt in the land of Nod, east of Eden.

The Flood

1. Men began to multiply on the earth, and God saw their wickedness was great. Only Noe, a just man, found favor with the Lord. And God said to Noe, "Make an ark, for I will bring a great flood upon the earth to destroy all flesh. But I will establish my covenant with thee, and thou shalt enter the ark with thy family.

2. "And," the Lord said, "of every living creature thou shalt bring two into the ark, male and female, that they may live." Noe did all that God had commanded. Then he and his sons—Sem, Ham, and Japheth—his wife, and his sons' wives went into the ark to escape the flood. After seven days the waters came upon the earth.

3. The flood continued forty days. The waters rose above the mountains, so that they were covered. And every living thing on the earth was wiped out, from man to beast, from reptile to bird. Only Noe and those with him in the ark were left.

4. After a hundred and fifty days the waters subsided and the ark rested on the mountains of Ararat. Forty days later Noe released a dove but she returned, for water covered the whole earth.

5. After seven days again he sent her forth and she came back with an olive leaf. Noe knew the waters had abated.

6. Then God told Noe to go out of the ark with his family, and bring out every living thing he had with him. When they had come out, Noe built an altar to the Lord and made an offering. Then the Lord said, "I will never again destroy every living creature." And He set the rainbow in the clouds as a token of His pledge.

The Tower of Babel

1. Noe's descendants increased rapidly. All still used the same language.

2. They discovered a valley in Babylonia and settled there. Then they said, "Let us make bricks and build a city, and a tower with its top in the heavens."

3. But the Lord said, "This is only the beginning of what they will do. Hereafter they will not be restrained from anything." And He changed their language so that——

4. —they spoke in different tongues, and He scattered them over the earth; and they stopped building the city. For this reason it was called Babel—"Confusion."

Abraham, founder of a nation

1. The Lord now chose a man, Abraham, to be the father of a great nation. "Leave thy country," the Lord said, "for the land I will show thee. In thee shall all the nations of the earth be blessed." So Abraham took Sara, his wife, and Lot, his brother's son——

2. —and journeyed to find the Promised Land. But there was strife between their herdsmen, and so they separated. Abraham went and settled in Chanaan.

3. Abraham and his wife were childless, but one day the Lord promised him an heir. At the Lord's command, Abraham made a burnt offering. When the sun had set—

4. —a flame shot out from the smoking oven. And God made a covenant, promising the land of Chanaan to Abraham and his descendants. Later three strangers came to Abraham's tent and he gave them food. Then he heard from one of them the words of the Lord: "Sara, thy wife, shall have a son." But Sara laughed, for she and Abraham were old.

Abraham and Isaac

1. As the Lord had promised, Sara bore Abraham a son in his old age, and Abraham called him Isaac. Then, one day, God put Abraham to a test. "Take thy only son Isaac," God said; "go into the district of Moria and offer him as a sacrifice on the hill I shall point out." So Abraham set out with Isaac and two servants, and cut wood for the offering.

2. When they arrived at the hill, Isaac said to his father Abraham, "Father!" He answered, "Yes, son?" Isaac said, "Father, thou hast the fire and the wood

3. "—but where is the sheep for the burnt offering?" "God Himself will provide the sheep, my son," Abraham answered. Then he built an altar and bound his son Isaac.

4. Abraham laid him on the wood upon the altar and took the knife to kill him. But an angel called to him, "Lay not thy hand upon the boy! I know now thou fearest God, since thou hast not spared thy only son."

5. Then Abraham looked up and saw a ram caught by its horns in the bush, and he offered it in place of his son.

Isaac and Rebecca

1. When Abraham was well advanced in years, he sent his oldest servant to obtain a wife for Isaac in the city in Mesopotamia where Abraham's brother Nahor lived.

2. The servant rested his camels near the well outside the city. Rebecca, the beautiful grand-daughter of Nahor, came with a jar and gave water to all.

3. When Rebecca's family heard how the Lord had guided the servant, they said, "Take Rebecca and let her be married to thy master's son, as the Lord has decided."

4. And Rebecca and her maids mounted the camels and followed the servant. Now Isaac went out in the field for a walk. He looked up and saw the camels approaching.

5. "It is my master," the servant said, and Rebecca covered herself with her veil. After the servant had told Isaac all he had done, Isaac took her to wife.

Isaac's twin sons

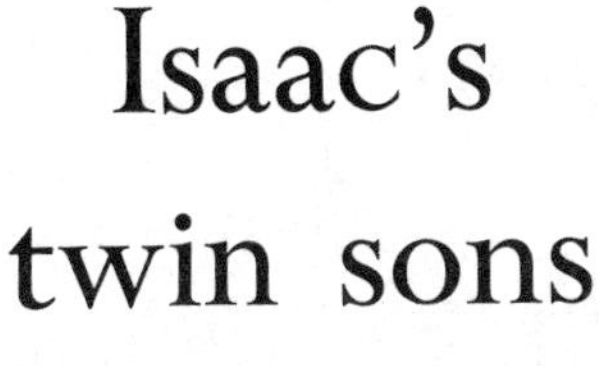

1. Isaac and Rebecca had twin sons, Esau and Jacob. Esau was a hunter, Jacob a shepherd.

2. Once when Jacob was cooking, Esau came in from the field famished. Jacob gave him some bread and lentils in exchange for his birthright. When Isaac was old——

3. —and his eyesight had failed, he begged Esau for some game, and promised his blessing. After Esau had gone hunting, Rebecca sent Jacob in with savory food——

4. —having putting on him the clothes of Esau and, on his hands and neck, the skin of kids, so he would be hairy like Esau. Isaac, deceived, gave him Esau's blessing.

5. When Esau returned from hunting and heard what had happened, he cried, "He took my birthright and now he has taken my blessing!" He swore to kill Jacob.

Jacob's vision

Rebecca urged Jacob to flee to her brother Laban until Esau's fury should subside. So he set out. That night he slept in the open with a stone for a pillow. He dreamed that a ladder was set up on the ground, with its top reaching to heaven; angels of God were ascending and descending on it. The Lord stood beside him and said, "I am the Lord, the God of Abraham, thy father, and the God of Isaac. I will give thee and thy descendants the land on which thou liest. Thou shalt spread abroad to the west, to the east, to the north, and to the south. I will be with thee and protect thee wherever thou goest." When Jacob woke, he said, "Truly the Lord is in this place and I did not know it." He took the stone he had placed under his head, set it up as a memorial pillar, and poured oil on it. He called the place Bethel, "The House of God."

Jacob's family

1. Jacob continued his journey and came to the land of Laban. There he met Rachel, the daughter of Laban, when she brought her father's flock to be watered.

2. Jacob loved Rachel. To win her, he worked seven years for Laban. But Laban tricked Jacob into marrying her sister Lia first. Jacob had twelve sons——

3. —who became the fathers of Israel's twelve tribes: Ruben, Simeon, Levi, Juda, Dan, Nephthali, Gad, Aser, Issachar, Zabulon, Joseph, and Benjamin.

4. One day the Lord said to Jacob, "Return to thy kin; I will be with thee." So Jacob mounted his family on camels, took all his herds, and went to Chanaan. On the way God blessed him and gave him a new name—"Israel"; his descendants were called Israelites. When Esau saw Jacob, he ran to him and embraced him, and they wept.

Joseph the dreamer

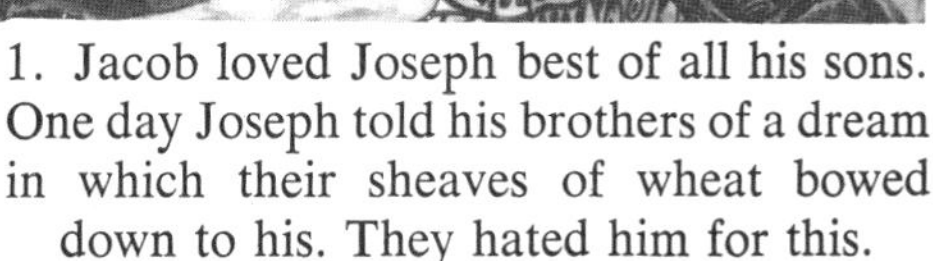

1. Jacob loved Joseph best of all his sons. One day Joseph told his brothers of a dream in which their sheaves of wheat bowed down to his. They hated him for this.

2. So they plotted to kill him. They stripped him and threw him into a cistern in the desert. But when a caravan of traders passed, the brothers sold him instead.

3. Then, after killing a goat, they dipped Joseph's tunic in the blood and sent someone with it to their father.

4. Jacob thought a wild beast had devoured Joseph, and mourned many days. Meanwhile the traders sold Joseph in Egypt to Phutiphar, captain of Pharao's guard.

Joseph in prison

1. Joseph found favor with Phutiphar, who placed him in charge of his household and all his property.

2. But Phutiphar's wife became angry with Joseph.

3. She lied about him to her husband, who committed him to prison, where were also Pharao's chief butler and chief baker.

4. One night the butler dreamed of a vine with three branches; from their grapes he squeezed juice into Pharao's cup.

5. The same night the baker dreamed he had three baskets on his head; in the top one was every kind of baked food for Pharao, but birds were eating it.

6. Joseph said the butler's dream meant that in three days he would serve Pharao again; the baker's, that in three days Pharao would hang him. And so it was.

Ruler in Egypt

1. Two years afterward, Pharao was troubled by two dreams. In the first, seven cows, sleek and fat, came out of the Nile and browsed; after them came seven thin cows and devoured the fat ones. In the second dream, seven fat ears of grain grew on one stalk——

2. —but after them sprouted seven more ears, thin and blasted by the wind, that swallowed up the fat ears.

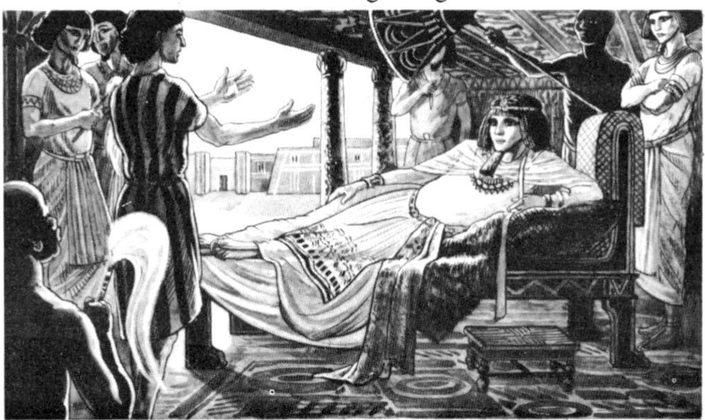

3. Then the butler remembered Joseph, and they brought him quickly out of the dungeon to interpret the dreams. Joseph said, "Seven years of plenty will come, but there will follow seven years of famine."

4. Joseph advised Pharao to select a wise man to collect food and store it up against the years of famine. "Behold, I appoint thee over the whole land," Pharao said.

5. So Joseph collected the fc d of the years of plenty and stored it. When the famine spread, he opened the store-houses and people came from everywhere to buy grain.

Joseph forgives his brothers

1. Joseph's brothers, too, came to buy grain in Egypt, but they did not recognize him.

2. Then Joseph ordered them to bring to Egypt the youngest brother, Benjamin, who had stayed at home with Jacob. Simeon he bound and kept with him.

3. But Jacob, fearful, said, "Benjamin shall not go with you." When they were emptying their sacks, they found their money with the grain and were dismayed.

4. It was Joseph who had put back their money. When they had eaten all the grain, they had to go back to Egypt, with Benjamin, to buy more. Joseph feasted them.

5. And, seeing Benjamin, he wept. On their way home, Joseph's steward overtook them and found their money in each sack again, and, in Benjamin's, Joseph's silver cup.

6. Terrified, they returned to Joseph's house. "The one with whom the cup was found will be my slave," Joseph said; "as for the rest, go in peace." Juda offered to stay in place of Benjamin, saying that if the boy did not go home his father would die——

7. —as he had already lost one of his sons. At this, Joseph could not control himself. He wept aloud. "I am your brother Joseph," he said, "whom you sold into Egypt. Do not be distressed. Not you but God sent me here." He kissed all his brothers and told them to bring Jacob and their families to Egypt, where he would provide for them.

8. The sons of Jacob brought their father, their little ones, their wives, and their herds to Egypt. Pharao greeted them and told Joseph to settle them in Gesen.

9. When Jacob was very old, he died, after blessing his twelve sons and foretelling that the Messias would be born of the tribe of one of them, Juda.

Moses, prince and shepherd

1. Joseph and that whole generation died. The Israelites became numerous, and a new Pharao forced them into slavery. When they still increased, Pharao commanded, "Throw into the river every boy born to the Jews." But one Hebrew woman——

2. —put her son in a papyrus basket and placed it among reeds on the river's bank. Pharao's daughter found it. She adopted the boy, and called him Moses.

3. Moses, grown up, saw an Egyptian striking a Hebrew. He slew the Egyptian, then fled to Madian, where he married and tended sheep in the desert.

4. One day God, speaking from a flaming bush, summoned him to lead the Israelites out of Egypt into the Promised Land. His brother Aaron was to be his spokesman.

5. Moses started back to Egypt. There he and Aaron assembled the Israelites, and Aaron told them everything the Lord had said to Moses. They bowed down in worship.

The Passover

1. But Pharao would not let the Israelites go, although God brought nine plagues upon Egypt. Then, at God's command, Moses told each Israelite family to slay a lamb.

2. They dipped a bunch of herbs in the blood and sprinkled their doorposts with it. Then, ready to depart, they ate the roasted flesh with unleavened bread and herbs.

3. At midnight the Lord slew every first-born of men and animals in the land, but passed over the houses of the Israelites. There was loud wailing throughout Egypt.

4. During the night, Pharao and the Egyptians urged the Israelites to depart at once, and gave them gold and silver. So they set out with their flocks and herds. And God ordered them to celebrate the Passover and the departure throughout their generations.

The Red Sea

1. The Israelites marched out of Egypt toward the Red Sea. By day a column of cloud showed them the way, by night a column of fire. They encamped by the sea.

2. But Pharao changed his mind and pursued the Israelites with his whole army. When the Israelites saw the Egyptians, they cried out to the Lord in great fright.

3. The Lord told Moses to lift his staff over the sea. And a strong east wind swept the sea and divided the water. The Israelites marched through the midst of the sea —

4. —on dry land. The Egyptians followed but the Lord so clogged their chariot wheels that they could hardly drive.

5. Then the Lord told Moses to stretch out his staff again. The water flowed back and covered Pharao's whole army.

God gives Moses the

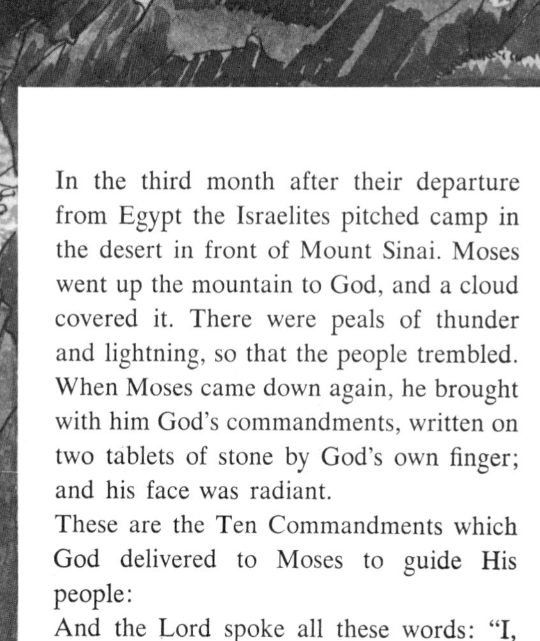

In the third month after their departure from Egypt the Israelites pitched camp in the desert in front of Mount Sinai. Moses went up the mountain to God, and a cloud covered it. There were peals of thunder and lightning, so that the people trembled. When Moses came down again, he brought with him God's commandments, written on two tablets of stone by God's own finger; and his face was radiant.

These are the Ten Commandments which God delivered to Moses to guide His people:

And the Lord spoke all these words: "I, the Lord, am your God, Who brought you out of the land of Egypt, that place of slavery.

1. *You shall not have other gods besides Me.*

2. *You shall not carve idols for yourselves in the shape of anything in the sky above or on the earth below or in the waters beneath the earth; you shall not bow down before them or worship them. For I, the Lord, your God, am a jealous God, inflicting punishment for their father's wickedness on the children of those who hate Me, down to the third and fourth generation; but bestowing mercy down to the thousandth generation, on the children of those who love Me and keep My commandments.*

Ten Commandments

3. *You shall not take the name of the Lord, your God, in vain. For the Lord will not leave unpunished him who takes His name in vain.*

4. *Remember to keep holy the Sabbath day. Six days you may labor and do all your work, but the seventh day is the Sabbath of the Lord, your God. No work may be done then either by you, or your son or daughter, or your male or female slave, or your beast, or by the alien who lives with you. In six days the Lord made the heavens and the earth, the sea and all that is in them; but on the seventh day He rested. That is why the Lord has blessed the Sabbath day and made it holy.*

5. *Honor your father and your mother, that you may have a long life in the land which the Lord, your God, is giving you.*

6. *You shall not kill.*

7. *You shall not commit adultery.*

8. *You shall not steal.*

9. *You shall not bear false witness against your neighbor.*

10. *You shall not covet your neighbor's house. You shall not covet your neighbor's wife, nor his male or female slave, nor his ox or ass, nor anything else that belongs to him."*

Scouts visit the land of milk and honey

1. Moses sent twelve scouts into the land of Chanaan, which the Lord had said He was giving the Israelites. There they cut down a branch with a single cluster of grapes so heavy that two of them carried it on a pole, as well as pomegranates and figs. After forty days they returned, met the Israelites in the desert, and showed them the fruit.

2. "The land flows with milk and honey," they reported. "However, the people are fierce, and the towns fortified." At this the Israelites wailed and grumbled.

3. When Josue and Caleb, two of the scouts, said, "If the Lord is pleased with us He will give us that land," they threatened to stone them. But at the Meeting Tent——

4. —the glory of God appeared, and the Lord declared those who doubted would die in the desert. Only their little ones and Josue and Caleb would enter the Land.

5. So for forty years they wandered in the desert. On the borders of the Promised Land, Aaron gave up his priestly garments to his son Eleazar and died.

Balaam's ass

1. Now the Israelites marched into the country east of the Jordan and won great victories. So Balac, King of Moab, sent princes to Balaam, a famous prophet, summoning him to come and curse the Israelites. But the Lord refused to let him come.

2. Balac again sent princes, and now Balaam went with them. As he was riding, his ass saw an angel, with sword drawn, and turned off the road. Balaam beat her.

3. Then Balaam, too, saw the angel of the Lord and bowed to the ground. "Go with the men," the angel said, "but say only what I tell thee." So Balaam went on.

4. Balac took Balaam to a high place. From there he saw the Israelite clans. "Build me seven altars here," the prophet ordered. On these Balac laid offerings.

5. But when he asked Balaam to curse the Israelites, the prophet could only bless them, saying, "A star shall rise out of Israel, and a scepter strike Moab."

The fall of Jericho

1. The Israelites waged war against the Madianites and defeated them. After this, Moses blessed the people and went up Mount Nebo, where the Lord showed him the Promised Land. Then he died and Josue became leader, as the Lord had commanded.

2. Josue sent spies across the Jordan. In Jericho, Rahab, a woman whose house was on the city wall, lodged them. She let them down with a rope when danger threatened.

3. They reported to Josue, who moved with all the Israelites to the Jordan. The priests, carrying the Ark, went in first; the waters parted and the people crossed.

4. As a memorial, twelve stones from the bed of the Jordan were set up. Then the Israelites celebrated the Passover—their first in the Promised Land.

5. When Josue was near Jericho, he raised his eyes and saw an angel facing him, sword in hand. "I am the captain of the host of the Lord," the angel told him. Then Josue learned that the Lord would deliver Jericho into his power. As the Lord ordered——

6. —the Israelites circled the city once each day for six days, with the Ark and seven priests blowing rams' horns. On the seventh day they marched around seven times and then raised a tremendous shout. The wall collapsed, and the Israelites stormed the city and burned it, putting to the sword everyone except Rahab and her family.

The conquering host

1. Now Josue sent about three thousand fighting men to attack the city of Hai, but they were defeated. Hearing this, Josue and the elders tore their garments.

2. Before the Ark of the Lord they put dust upon their heads. "Alas, O Lord God," Josue prayed, "why wouldst Thou bring our people over the Jordan to destroy us?"

3. Then the Lord told Josue an Israelite had sinned against Him by putting goods taken from Jericho into his baggage. In Achan's tent gold and silver were found.

4. All Israel stoned him to death. Then Josue mustered the army and went up to Hai. When the army of Hai came out, the Israelites fled in seeming defeat, and all the enemy pursued them. But now other Israelites rose from an ambush west of the city and captured it.

5. Later Josue built an altar on Mount Ebal and, after sacrifice, inscribed the Law of Moses upon stones for all to see.

6. The Israelites were tricked into an alliance with the city of Gabaon. Soon five southern kings marched against it.

7. When the men of Gabaon sent for help, Josue made a surprise attack and routed the enemy. While they fled, the Lord killed many more with hailstones.

8. After Josue had conquered the south, the northern kings marched against him with all their troops. The Israelites attacked them at the waters of Merom.

9. Josue captured all the kings and their cities, and put them to the sword. Then he divided their lands among the tribes.

10. When Josue was old, he summoned all the tribes and reminded them to serve the Lord sincerely. Shortly afterwards he died.

Death of a tyrant

1. Some years later the Israelites offended the Lord. He allowed them to fall into the power of the Chanaanite King, Jabin, whose general, Sisara, oppressed them. Then the prophetess Debora summoned Barac and told him to go to Mount Thabor with ten thousand men, and she would deliver Sisara and his troops into his power.

2. "If thou wilt come with me, I will go," Barac answered, so Debora went with him and the Israelites. Now Sisara assembled his forces at the Wadi Cison, and the Israelites swooped down upon them from Mount Thabor. And the Lord put Sisara and all his chariots and all his forces to rout before Barac.

3. Sisara fled on foot to the tent of Jahel, whom he thought friendly. She welcomed him in and gave him milk to drink——

4. —and covered him with a rug. But while he slept she drove a tent peg through his temple. Thus God humbled the Chanaanites.

Gedeon saves Israel

1. After forty years of peace, the Madianites came into the land of Israel, destroying and stealing. But an angel appeared to Gedeon, and said, "O champion, go and save Israel!" As a sign, he touched Gedeon's offering of meat and cakes; fire consumed them.

2. Later, when Gedeon put a fleece on the ground, it was wet with dew when the ground was dry——

3. —and dry when there was dew on the ground. Gedeon knew now the Lord was going to save Israel through him. From soldiers sent by the tribes he selected three hundred and provided them with horns, jars, and torches. In the dark——

4. —they surrounded the enemy camp. At Gedeon's signal, they blew the horns, broke the jars, and cried out, "A sword for the Lord and Gedeon!" The whole camp fell to running, shouting, and fleeing, and the Israelites pursued them beyond the Jordan.

Jephte's daughter

1. Some time later, the Ammonites warred on Israel. The elders went to Jephte, an outlaw chieftain, and begged him to take command of the Israelite army.

2. They swore that he should be their prince. Before the battle, Jephte vowed that if he won he would sacrifice whoever first came out of his house on his return.

3. Jephte inflicted a severe defeat on the Ammonites. But when he returned to his house, his daughter, an only child, came forth, playing the tambourines and dancing.

4. Then he tore his garments and, groaning, told her of the vow he had made. She answered, "My father, do unto me what thou hast promised, since the victory has been granted."
And it became a custom for Israelite women yearly to mourn Jephte's daughter.

The story of Samson

1. Samson was an Israelite blessed with great strength. When a lion came roaring upon him, he killed it with his bare hands.

2. Later, finding a swarm of bees and honey in the carcass, he made a riddle: "Out of the eater came forth food; out of the strong, sweetness," which he asked at his wedding banquet. His Philistine guests (their nation now ruled Israel) could not solve it till his Philistine wife coaxed the answer from him. Afterward she married another.

3. In revenge, Samson burned the Philistines' harvest. So the Philistines made war on Juda. The Jews bound Samson——

4. —to deliver him to the enemy, but he snapped the ropes. Then, with an ass's jawbone, he killed a thousand Philistines.

5. Samson fell in love with another Philistine woman, Dalila. She persuaded him to tell her the secret of his strength: that he was consecrated to God as a Nazirite and had never allowed a razor to touch his head. So, while he slept, Dalila called for a man to shave off his hair. Then the Philistines gouged out Samson's eyes.

6. They put him in prison, where his hair began to grow again. When the Philistines made merry in the temple of their god Dagon, they called Samson to amuse them. He asked the attendant who led him to put him where he could touch the two middle columns of the temple. Then he pushed hard, and the temple fell, killing everybody inside.

Ruth

1. There was a famine in the land, so a man named Elimelech went with his wife, Noemi, into Moab. There his two sons married Moabite women——

2 —one named Orpha, the other Ruth. But the father and the sons died, and Noemi made ready to go back home when she heard her people had food again. Orpha kissed her good-by; but Ruth said, "Where thou shalt go, I will go; where thou shalt dwell, I also will dwell. Thy people shall be my people, and thy God my God."

3. They arrived in Bethlehem at harvest-time. Ruth went out to glean ears of grain left by the harvesters, in a field belonging to Booz, of the clan of Elimelech.

4. Booz saw Ruth and favored her. He took her as his wife and she bore a son, Obed. Obed was the father of Jesse, and Jesse became the father of David.

Samuel the prophet

1. Anna, wife of Elcana of Ramathaim-Sophim, went to the temple at Silo and prayed, "O Lord, if Thou wilt give to Thy servant a man child, I will give him to the Lord."

2. The Lord remembered her, and Anna bore a son, Samuel. She brought him to the priest Heli at Silo, to serve God in the temple; and the child pleased the Lord.

3. One night, when Samuel slept in the temple, where the Ark was, the Lord called him. Samuel ran to Heli and said, "Here am I, for thou didst call me."

4. "I did not call," Heli answered. "Go back and sleep." Three times the Lord called Samuel; then Heli understood that He wished to speak to the boy.

5. The fourth time, Samuel answered, "Speak, Lord, for Thy servant heareth." Then God told him the sons of Heli were wicked, and they would be punished.

6. Samuel later became a prophet. Then Heli's sons carried the Ark off to war.

7. They were killed, and the Ark was taken. When Heli heard this, he died.

8. The Philistines, who had taken the Ark, brought it into the temple of Dagon. The next day, they found the statue of Dagon lying on its face, on the ground before the Ark. They set it up again; but in the morning, they found the statue on the ground again, and the head and hands cut off. Then deadly plagues smote them.

9. So they brought back the Ark. Now the Israelites put away the idols they had been worshipping and confessed they had sinned. When the Philistines came against them—

10. —the Lord heard Samuel's prayer and the enemy was overthrown. And Samuel set up a memorial stone—"the Stone of Help"—saying, "Thus far the Lord has helped us."

Saul is chosen king

1. When Samuel was old, the elders of Israel said, "Give us a king to judge us and go out before us, and fight our battles for us."

2. Now Saul, son of Cis, took a servant and went seeking his father's lost asses. Hearing there was a seer in the city, he came to Samuel for help.

3. The Lord had revealed to Samuel that Saul was to be ruler over Israel; and the next day Samuel poured oil upon Saul's head and said, "The Lord has anointed thee."

4. Samuel called together the people to Maspha and showed them Saul, who stood head and shoulders above them. And all cried, "God save the King!"

5. They made Saul king at Galgal. Then he led the people against the Philistines. But when they saw the enemy host, they hid themselves in caves and thickets.

Jonathan and the Philistines

1. Jonathan, son of Saul, said to his armor-bearer, "Let us go over to the garrison of the Philistines. It is easy for the Lord to save by many or by few."

2. So both of them showed themselves to the Philistines, who cried, "Behold, the Hebrews come out of their holes! Come up to us, and we will show you a thing."

3. Jonathan went up, creeping on his hands and feet, and his armor-bearer after him. And some fell before Jonathan, others his armor-bearer slew—about twenty in all.

4. Then there was a miracle in the camp. The earth trembled, and the Philistines flew this way and that. Every man's sword was turned upon his neighbor when——

5. —Saul and all the Israelites joined in the fight. There was great slaughter and they chased the foe as far as Bethaven. Thus God saved Israel that day.

David the shepherd

1. But Saul did evil in the eyes of the Lord; and Samuel told him the Lord had rejected him.

2. Then God sent Samuel to Bethlehem to find a king among the sons of a man called Jesse. When Jesse brought seven sons before Samuel, he asked if there were any others. "There remains yet a young one, who keeps the sheep." "Send and fetch him," Samuel answered. So David was brought in; he was ruddy and beautiful to behold.

3. And Samuel anointed David in the midst of his brethren, for the Lord had said, "This is he."

4. The Spirit of the Lord came upon David, from that day. But an evil spirit troubled Saul, so he sent for David, who was a skillful musician; whenever David played his harp, the evil spirit departed.

David and Goliath

1. Now the Philistines came. Their champion, a giant named Goliath, challenged Israel. David said to King Saul:

2. "I will fight him." "Thou art but a boy," Saul replied. But David told him that he had killed a lion and a bear which had attacked his father's sheep.

3. "The Lord be with thee," said Saul, and David went forth. He chose five stones out of a brook and put them in his shepherd's bag; and he took a sling in his hand.

4. When Goliath beheld the young David, he despised him. But David cried, "I come in the name of the Lord!" And he took a stone and cast it with the sling.

5. It struck the Philistine on the forehead, and he fell on his face upon the earth. Then David ran up, drew Goliath's sword, and slew him and cut off his head.

Saul's jealousy

1. When David returned after Israel had defeated the Philistines, the women came out of the cities singing, "Saul slew his thousands and David his ten thousands."

2. Saul was very angry. The day after, while David played for the King, Saul threw a spear at him, but David stepped aside. And Saul feared David because the Lord was with him.

3. When David and his men killed two hundred Philistines, Saul gave him Michel, his daughter, to wife. Yet still Saul wanted to kill him.

4. Jonathan, Saul's son, loved David. He gave him his coat, sword, and bow, and told Saul good things about him. But when Saul threw his spear at David again——

5. —David fled to his house. Saul sent his guards to kill him, but Michel let him down through a window and laid an image on his bed to deceive them.

6. Jonathan failed to make peace, and by an arrow signal warned David against Saul.

7. So David fled to the cave of Odollam, where four hundred outlaws joined him.

8. Saul took three thousand men and set out after David. He went to sleep in the very cave where David and his men lay hidden. David secretly cut off the hem of Saul's robe, but did not lay a hand upon the King. Later David showed him the hem. Saul wept. "May the Lord reward thee!" he said. "I know thou shalt surely be king."

9. Again, David found Saul sleeping in his tent; still he did not kill him, but took his spear and cup. Then, standing on a hill far off, he showed them to the King.

10. Fearing he would one day fall into Saul's hands, David fled to the Philistines, where King Achis welcomed him and his men. Achis went to war against Israel.

The death of Saul

1. Now Samuel was dead, and Saul, afraid of the Philistines, went to consult a witch at Endor.

2. "Bring up Samuel's spirit," he ordered. And Samuel appeared and said, "The Lord will give thy kingdom to David; tomorrow thou and thy sons shall be with me."

3. The Philistine princes did not want David to fight for them, fearing he would go over to Saul's side. So Achis sent him back to the land of the Philistines.

4. The Philistines fought against the men of Israel, who fled before them. Jonathan and two of his brothers were slain. Then the Philistine archers overtook Saul.

5. Saul, grievously wounded, said to his armor-bearer, "Kill me, lest they slay me and mock me." But he would not, so Saul took his own sword and fell upon it.

The capture of Jerusalem

1. After Saul's death, David was anointed King of the House of Juda at Hebron.

2. But Abner, Saul's general, made Isboseth, Saul's son, King of Israel. Then there was a very fierce battle at Gabaon, and the men of Israel were put to flight by the men of David.

3. "Make a league with me and I will bring to thee all Israel," Abner proposed to David, who agreed. But Abner was slain.

4. Isboseth, too, met his death. All the tribes of Israel anointed David their king, and made a league with him at Hebron.

5. Then he marched to Jerusalem. The Jebusites, the inhabitants of the land, cried, "David shall not come in!" Offering a reward to whoever should strike the Jebusites, David stormed the city and took it.

King David

1. The King dwelt in Jerusalem and called it "the city of David." Later he brought the Ark to the city with joyful shouting and sound of trumpet, himself leaping and dancing before the procession. He wanted to build a temple for the Ark, but the prophet Nathan told him it was the will of God that this work be done by his son.

2. Afterward David married Bethsabee, widow of Urias the Hethite, and she bore him a son, Solomon.

3. David, whom the Lord had taken out of the pastures from following the sheep to be ruler over Israel, reigned for forty years, doing justice to the people and winning great victories in war.

"The Lord is my Shepherd"

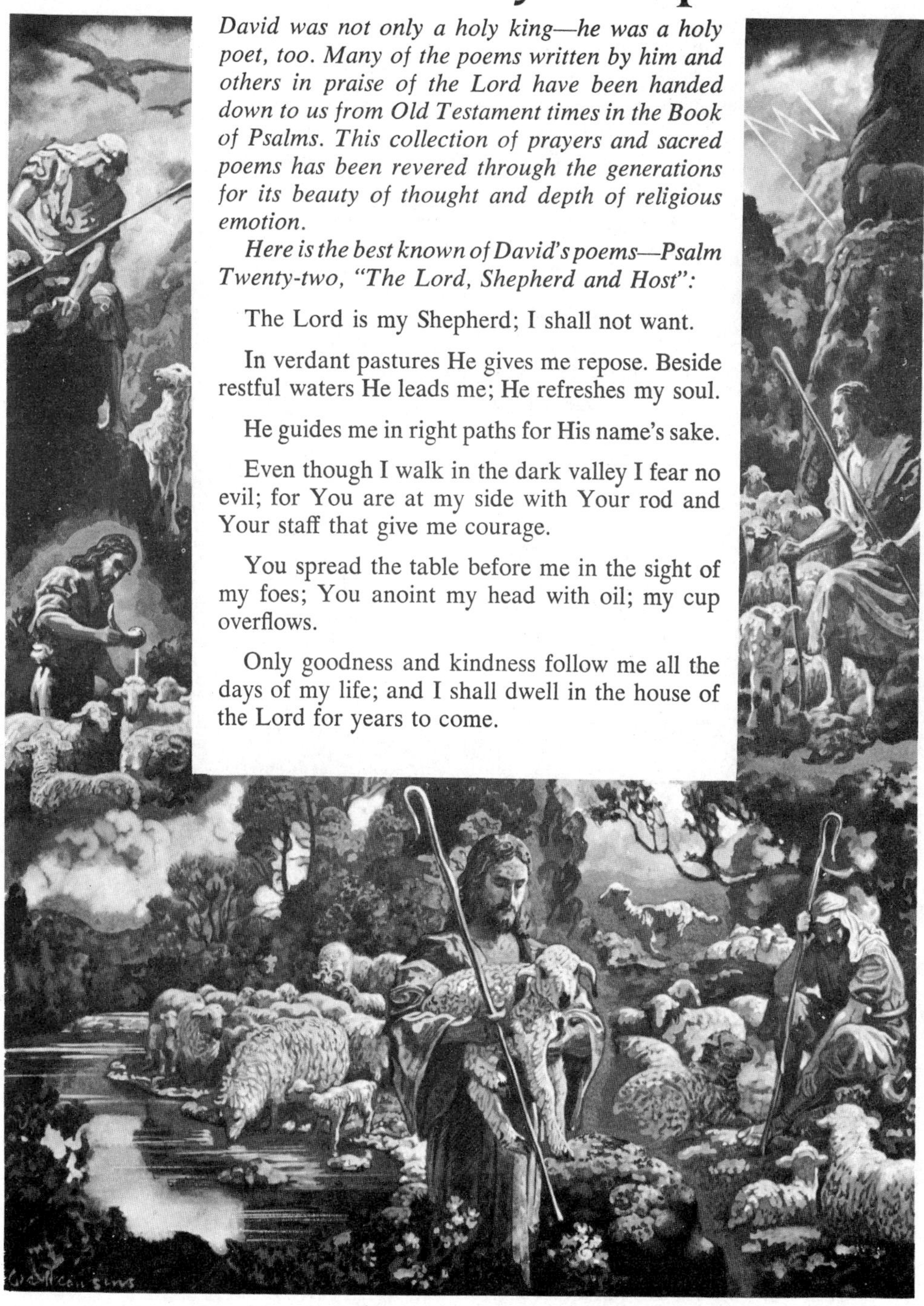

David was not only a holy king—he was a holy poet, too. Many of the poems written by him and others in praise of the Lord have been handed down to us from Old Testament times in the Book of Psalms. This collection of prayers and sacred poems has been revered through the generations for its beauty of thought and depth of religious emotion.

Here is the best known of David's poems—Psalm Twenty-two, "The Lord, Shepherd and Host":

The Lord is my Shepherd; I shall not want.

In verdant pastures He gives me repose. Beside restful waters He leads me; He refreshes my soul.

He guides me in right paths for His name's sake.

Even though I walk in the dark valley I fear no evil; for You are at my side with Your rod and Your staff that give me courage.

You spread the table before me in the sight of my foes; You anoint my head with oil; my cup overflows.

Only goodness and kindness follow me all the days of my life; and I shall dwell in the house of the Lord for years to come.

"I lift up my eyes"

Psalm One Hundred and Twenty—"The Lord Our Guardian"—is one of the loveliest and most inspiring poems of solace ever written. It is the song of the traveler who confidently relies upon the Lord to keep him from harm.

I lift up my eyes toward the mountains; whence shall help come to me?

My help is from the Lord, Who made heaven and earth.

May He not suffer your foot to slip; may He not slumber Who guards you:

Indeed He neither slumbers nor sleeps, the Guardian of Israel.

The Lord is your Guardian; the Lord is your Shade; He is beside you at your right hand.

The sun shall not harm you by day, nor the moon by night.

The Lord will guard you from all evil; He will guard your life.

The Lord will guard your coming and your going, both now and forever.

The reign of Solomon

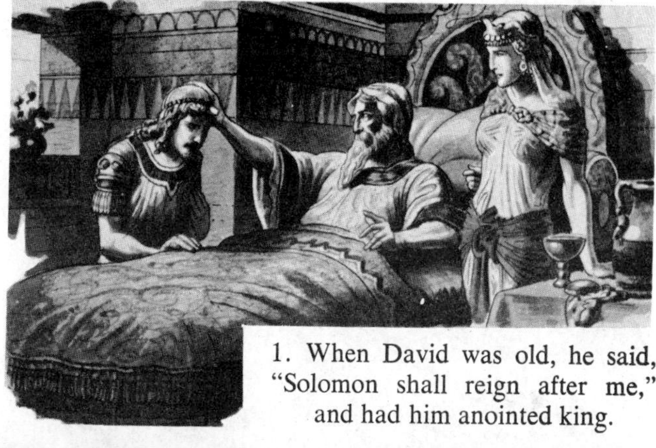

1. When David was old, he said, "Solomon shall reign after me," and had him anointed king.

2. Then David died, and Solomon sat upon the throne. God gave him wisdom, understanding, and largeness of heart, so that he was renowned in all nations. He built a Temple to the Lord, and in its sanctuary, or Holy of Holies, he set the Ark of the Lord, with the Ten Commandments in it. Solomon also built costly palaces for himself.

3. The Queen of Saba, hearing of the wisdom of Solomon, came to try him with hard questions. When she heard his wise answers, and saw the splendor of his household and the Temple, she cried, "Thy wisdom and thy works exceed the fame which I heard!" And she gave the King rich presents of gold, precious stones, and spices.

4. The wisdom of God was in Solomon. Once, two women came before the King with a child which each claimed as her own. "Bring me a sword," he ordered. "Divide the child in two and give half to each." "Give it to the other, do not kill it!" begged one of the women. "No," said Solomon, "give the child to this woman because she is the mother."

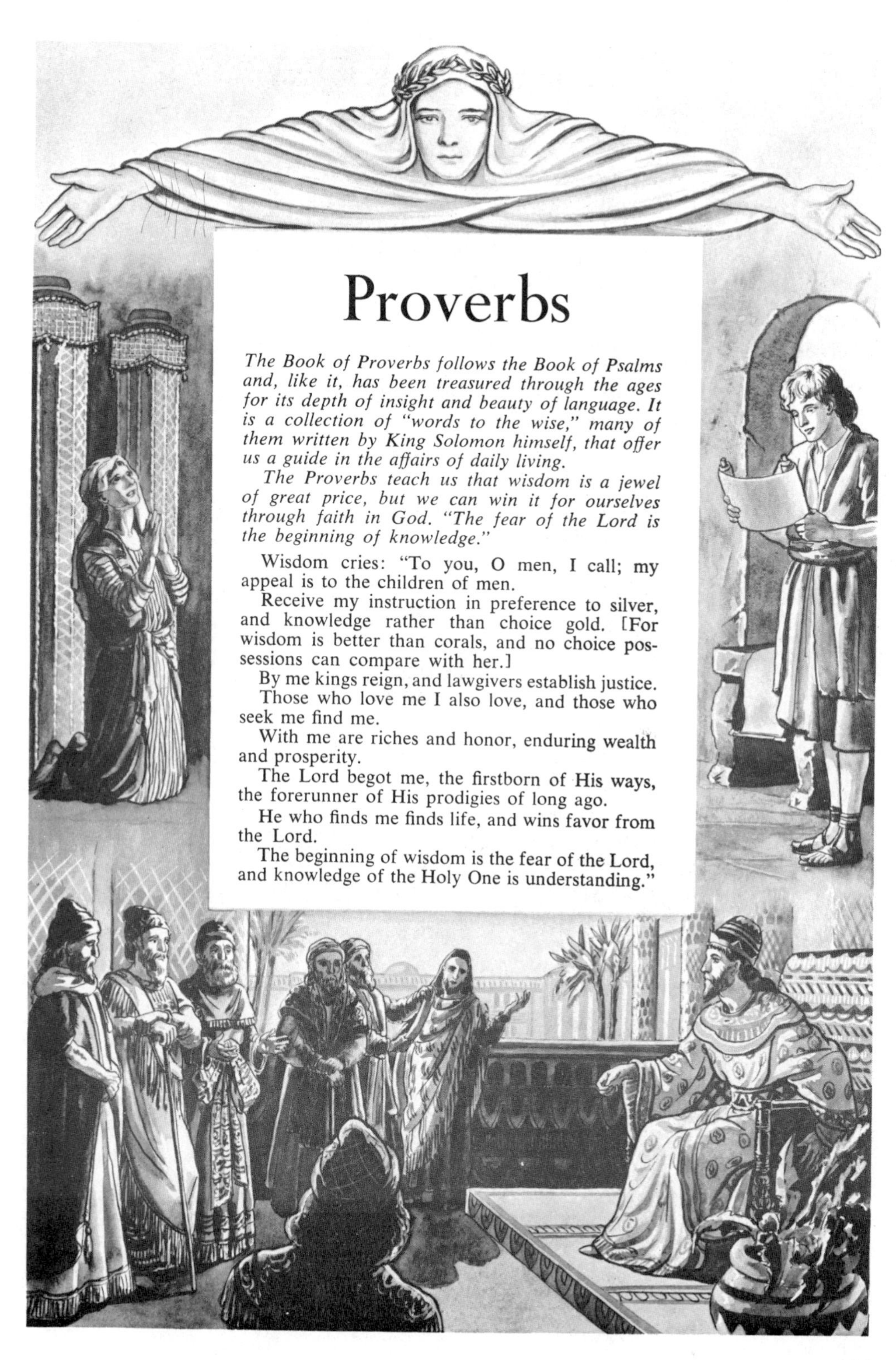

Proverbs

The Book of Proverbs follows the Book of Psalms and, like it, has been treasured through the ages for its depth of insight and beauty of language. It is a collection of "words to the wise," many of them written by King Solomon himself, that offer us a guide in the affairs of daily living.

The Proverbs teach us that wisdom is a jewel of great price, but we can win it for ourselves through faith in God. "The fear of the Lord is the beginning of knowledge."

Wisdom cries: "To you, O men, I call; my appeal is to the children of men.

Receive my instruction in preference to silver, and knowledge rather than choice gold. [For wisdom is better than corals, and no choice possessions can compare with her.]

By me kings reign, and lawgivers establish justice.

Those who love me I also love, and those who seek me find me.

With me are riches and honor, enduring wealth and prosperity.

The Lord begot me, the firstborn of His ways, the forerunner of His prodigies of long ago.

He who finds me finds life, and wins favor from the Lord.

The beginning of wisdom is the fear of the Lord, and knowledge of the Holy One is understanding."

Wise sayings

There are many more proverbs.

Here are some that lay stress on the simple virtues of character, honesty, and loving helpfulness in everyday life; and which emphasize that faith in God is more important than any other thing in the search for wise and selfless living.

A mild answer calms wrath, but a harsh word stirs up anger.

Better a little with fear of the Lord than a great fortune with anxiety.

Better a dish of herbs where love is than a fatted calf and hatred with it.

Pride goes before disaster and a haughty spirit before a fall.

Grandchildren are the crown of old men, and the glory of children is their parentage.

A good name is more desirable than great riches, and high esteem, than gold and silver.

The wicked man flees although no one pursues him; but the just man, like a lion, feels sure of himself.

Two things I ask of You, deny them not to me before I die:

Put falsehood and lying far from me, give me neither poverty nor riches [provide me only with the food I need;] lest, being full, I deny You, saying, "Who is the Lord?" or, being in want, I steal, and profane the name of my God.

Rival kingdoms

1. After Solomon died, his son Roboam reigned in his place. Then Jeroboam, a valiant man, came to the King with a multitude of people and asked him to make lighter the heavy yoke of labor and taxes that Solomon had put upon them.

2. Leaving his wise old counselors, Roboam hearkened to the young men that had been brought up with him. "I will add to your yoke," he told the people.

3. Israel revolted against the house of David. The ten tribes in the north made Jeroboam their king.

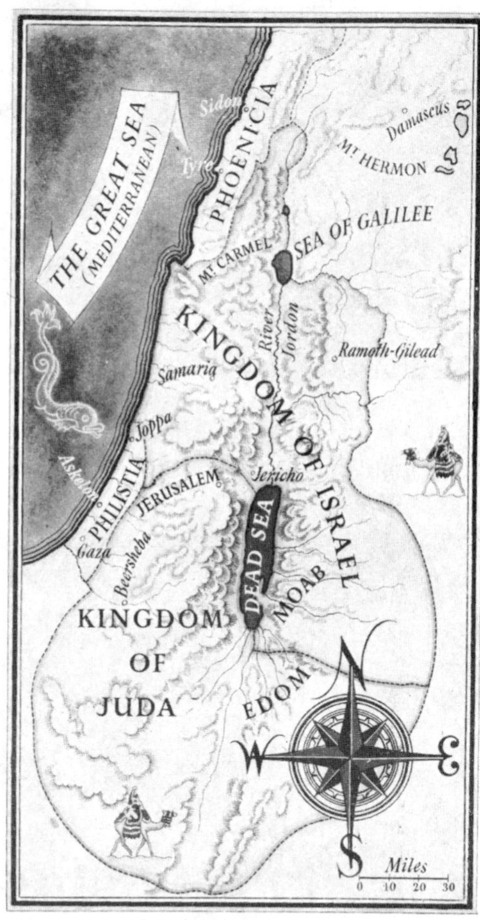

4. Only the tribes of Juda and Benjamin, in the south, followed Roboam, whose kingdom was centered on Jerusalem.

Elias the prophet

1. When King Achab of Israel set up an altar to Baal, the prophet Elias warned him——

2. —there would be a long drought. Then Elias hid near the torrent Carith, where ravens brought him food.

3. Later the torrent itself dried up, and God told Elias to go to Sarephtha and dwell with a widow there. She had only a handful of meal in her pot, but from the day he came it renewed itself and provided plenty

4. When the widow's son fell sick and died, Elias laid him upon his own bed and cried to the Lord. And the Lord heard his voice; the soul of the child returned.

5. "Thou art a man of God!" the mother exclaimed when Elias gave her back her son.

Yahweh or Baal

1. In the third year of the drought, King Achab and his steward traveled through the land to find grass for their perishing horses and mules. Elias met them, and Achab asked, "Art thou he that troublest Israel?" For he remembered the prophet's warning.

2. "Not I, but thou and thy father's house who follow Baal!" Elias answered. "Gather unto Mount Carmel all Israel and the prophets of Baal." There, Elias proposed that they test the powers of this false god and the Lord. A bullock was placed on Baal's altar, on wood, and his priests called on him to burn it. But Baal did not answer.

3. Then Elias built an altar to the Lord, and laid wood on it, and a bullock. Water was poured three times over all, till it ran round about the altar and filled a trench. Now Elias came near and prayed, "O Lord, show this day that Thou art the God of Israel!"

4. The fire of the Lord fell and consumed the offering, the wood, the stones, the dust; it licked up the water. When the people saw this, they fell on their faces and cried, "The Lord, He is God! The Lord, He is God!" "Take the prophets of Baal—let not one of them escape!" Elias ordered, and they were taken and killed.

5. Then Elias told his servant, "Go and look toward the sea." He saw only a little cloud arising; but soon the heavens grew dark with clouds and wind, and a great rain fell. Achab rode to the city in his chariot, and Elias ran before him.

"They seek my life!"

1. When Queen Jezabel, Achab's wicked wife, heard the priests of Baal had been slain, she threatened to take Elias' life. Elias fled into the desert, where he was miraculously fed; on the strength of that food he walked all the long way to a cave on Mount Horeb.

2. "What dost thou here, Elias?" the Lord asked him. "I alone am left of Thy prophets, and they seek my life!" he answered. "Stand upon the mount and behold the Lord passing," God said. And a great wind overthrew the mountains; then there was an earthquake, and after the earthquake a fire. But the Lord was not in the wind——

3. —nor in the earthquake, nor in the fire. But after the fire there was a whistling of a gentle air.

4. Elias covered his face, and the Lord told him to go his way; those who had worshipped Baal would be slain.

The calling of Eliseus

1. Departing from Horeb, Elias found Eliseus, who was ploughing, and cast his mantle upon him. Eliseus left his oxen.

2. He traveled with Elias and served him faithfully. Some years later, at Jericho, prophets told Eliseus, "This day the Lord will take thy master away."

3. The two went on together till they stood by the Jordan. Then Elias struck the waters with his mantle and they divided. Both men passed over on dry ground.

4. As they walked and talked together, a fiery chariot and horses parted them, and a whirlwind lifted Elias up to heaven. But his mantle fell, and Eliseus took it.

Stories of Eliseus

1. But Eliseus inherited more than Elias' mantle—people said, "The spirit of Elias rests upon him." Once a poor widow called to him, "The creditor is come to take away my sons to serve him!" "What hast thou in thy house?" Eliseus asked her.

2. She had only a jar of oil. On Eliseus' advice she borrowed many empty vessels—and miraculously filled them from her one jar! She was soon free from debt.

3. Again, a certain rich woman gave food and lodging to Eliseus. One day her son, in the field with his father and the reapers, cried, "My head aches!" And he fell.

4. At noon he died. But Eliseus, called by the mother, prayed, and raised the child to life.

5. When one of the faithful brought this man of God twenty loaves of barley and some corn, Eliseus told his servant, "Give it to the people, that they may eat." A hundred men ate—and there was food left over!

Naaman the leper

1. Naaman, general of the army of the King of Syria, was a great man, but a leper. One day his wife's maid, an Israelite girl taken captive by the Syrians, said to her mistress, "I wish my master had been with the prophet that is in Samaria——

2. "—for he would certainly have healed him!" Then Naaman went to his King, who sent him to King Joram of Israel, asking that the general be healed. The King of Israel feared Syria was seeking an excuse for a quarrel, but Eliseus sent a message: "Let him come to me, and let him know there is a prophet in Israel." So Naaman came——

3. —with his horses and chariots and stood at Eliseus' door. When the prophet sent a messenger saying, "Go and wash seven times in the Jordan, and thy flesh shall recover health," Naaman was angry. "I thought he would have come out and healed me!" he cried. "Are not the rivers of Damascus better than all the waters of Israel?"

4. But as he turned away, his servants said, "If the prophet had bid thee do some great thing, surely thou wouldst have done it. How much better is what he now has said to thee!" Naaman could not help but agree. He went down and washed in the Jordan seven times—and his flesh was restored, like the flesh of a little child.

5. Returning to the man of God with all his attendants, Naaman said, "In truth I know there is no other God in all the earth, but only in Israel. I beseech thee, take a present from me." Eliseus refused. "As thou wilt," Naaman said. "But I will henceforth not offer sacrifice to other gods, but to the Lord only."

Eliseus' chariots of fire

1. The Syrians made war on Israel, but Eliseus warned King Joram of their ambushes.

2. Hearing this, the King of Syria sent an army to capture Eliseus. But the prophet prayed, and chariots of fire stood around him. He prayed again——

3. —and the Lord struck the Syrians with blindness. Then he led them to King Joram and told him to let them go. Later another army besieged Samaria.

4. There was a great famine in the city. King Joram came to Eliseus, who prophesied there would soon be food enough.

5. That evening four lepers went to beg in the enemy camp and found the Syrians had fled, leaving their supplies behind.

Jehu, King of Israel

1. King Joram, son of wicked Queen Jezabel, was wounded in a fight with the Syrians, and returned to Jezrahel to be healed. Meanwhile, Eliseus had sent a prophet to anoint a new king over Israel, Jehu. Jehu and his men rode to Jezrahel in chariots.

2. When the tower watchman reported, "I see a troop!" Joram sent a messenger to learn if they came in peace. But neither this messenger returned, nor the next.

3. Now the watchman said, "The driving is furious, like Jehu's!" So Joram rode out and asked, "Is it peace, Jehu?" "Not so long as thy mother's sorceries exist!"

4. Joram turned to flee, but Jehu sent an arrow through his heart and went into the city. When Queen Jezabel called——

5. —from a window, Jehu cried to her servants, "Throw her down!" And the wall was sprinkled with her blood.

The boy-king of Juda

1. Ochozias, King of Juda, who had been with Joram, tried to flee from Jehu but was wounded and died. His mother, Athalia, a worshiper of Baal, seized the throne.

2. She slew all of Ochozias's sons but the baby Joas, who was saved by his aunt. The priest Joiada hid him in the Temple. Seven years later Joiada brought forth——

3. —the King's son, put the crown upon him, and anointed him king before the people and the soldiers. Approving, they cried, "God save the King!"

4. Athalia heard the noise and went into the Temple. Seeing the King, and all the people rejoicing, she tore her garments. "A conspiracy! A conspiracy!" she cried. But Joiada commanded the soldiers to take her out of the Temple and slay her.

A king and his arrows

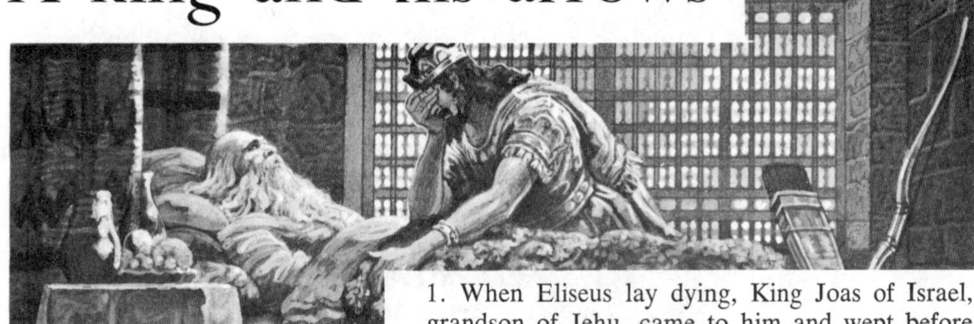

1. When Eliseus lay dying, King Joas of Israel, grandson of Jehu, came to him and wept before him. "Bring a bow and arrows," Eliseus said.

2. Eliseus put his hands over the King's hands on the bow. "Open the window to the east," he told the King. And when Joas had opened it, Eliseus said:

3. "Shoot an arrow." And he shot. "The arrow of the Lord's deliverance," Eliseus cried, "and the arrcw of the deliverance from Syria!" Then he ordered:

4. "Strike with an arrow upon the ground!" Joas struck three times. The man of God was angry. "If thou hadst smitten five or six or seven times, thou hadst destroyed Syria," he said. "But now three times shalt thou smite it." Then Eliseus died.

The prophet Amos

1. When Jeroboam II, the son of Joas, was King of Israel, the Lord sent Amos, a shepherd of Thecua, to proclaim His judgment on Israel.

2. Israel, Juda, and their neighbors were to be punished for their crimes, Amos prophesied. Because they had not kept the Lord's commandments, but had lived sinfully, crushed the poor, and taken bribes, the Lord had said, "I will turn your feasts into mourning and all your songs into lamentation!

3. "I will cause you to go into captivity beyond Damascus. I will sift the house of Israel among all nations, as corn is sifted in a sieve. Then I will bring back My people and they shall rebuild the abandoned cities and inhabit them."

Osee

1. At the same time as Amos, there was in northern Israel a prophet named Osee. He told, allegorically, of his marriage to a sinful woman (Israel) who bore him children.

2. One was called "Without mercy" and another "Not my people"—because the Lord would have no mercy on Israel, whose people were no longer His, Osee proclaimed.

3. Later Osee bought another sinful wife and told her, "Thou shalt wait for me many days." But this was all symbolic and meant that the children of Israel——

4. —would be for many years without king and without prince, and without sacrifice or altar. Thus Osee foretold that Israel——

5. —for her sins, would go into captivity. But he said God had told him, "I shall bring them back and love them freely."

Israel's captivity

1. Now the time of reckoning foretold by the prophets was at hand. Phacee, King of Israel, and Rasin, King of Syria, invaded Juda and laid siege to Jerusalem.

2. Achaz, King of Juda, disregarding the protests of the prophet Isaias, sent messengers to Theglathphalasar, King of the Assyrians, asking for help.

3. The Assyrian King slew Rasin and laid Damascus waste. But Achaz gave him silver and gold from the Temple, and paid him homage at Damascus.

4. When Osee followed Phacee as king, Salmanasar, the new ruler of Assyria, besieged Samaria, capital of Israel, for three years. Then the city fell, and the Israelites were taken to Assyria as captives and scattered through the land.

The vision of Isaias

1. Amos and Osee spoke to Israel in the north; the south had its prophet, too—Isaias—and he spoke to Juda. "In the year that King Ozias died," he said, "I saw the Lord.

2. "He was sitting upon a throne high and elevated. Above stood the seraphim with six wings. And they cried one to another, 'Holy, Holy, Holy—the Lord God of hosts, all the earth is full of His glory!' And the Temple shook, and was filled with smoke.

3. "And I said, 'Woe is me, because I am a man of unclean lips, and I dwell in the midst of a people that have unclean lips, and I have seen the Lord of hosts.'

4. "And one of the seraphim flew to me, and in his hand was a live coal, which he had taken with the tongs off the altar. He touched my mouth and said, 'Behold, this has touched thy lips, and thy iniquities shall be taken away, and thy sin shall be cleansed.' And I heard the voice of the Lord saying:

5. " 'Whom shall I send? And who shall go for us?' I said, 'Lo, here am I. Send me.' " Then God warned him, Isaias declared, that the land was to be made desolate, but a remnant of the people would be saved.

The prophecy of Isaias

1. And Isaias told the people of Juda, "The Lord will bring upon you the waters of a strong river—the King of the Assyrians, and all his might."

2. When Achaz was King, and sought the aid of Assyria against his enemies, Isaias warned him the Assyrians would make him their vassal. And so they did.

3. Twenty years passed, and now Ezechias, son of Achaz, reigned in Juda. He destroyed the pagan altars and idols, and did all that was good before the Lord.

4. He also rebelled against the Assyrians. So Sennacherib, King of Assyria, sent his officer Rabsaces with an army to Jerusalem. "Do you trust in your God?" Rabsaces cried. "Have any of the other gods delivered their lands from the Assyrians?"

5. Ezechias tore his garments in despair, but Isaias said, "Be not afraid."

6. When Ezechias received a letter from Sennacherib threatening to destroy Juda——

7. —he was fearful again, and went to the Temple to pray for help. Although the Assyrians were close at hand, Isaias prophesied the Lord would save Jerusalem. And that very night an angel of the Lord slew many thousands in the Assyrian camp. So Sennacherib returned to Assyria. As he was worshipping his god, two of his sons slew him.

8. Later, when Ezechias fell sick, the King of the Babylonians sent letters and presents to him. Pleased, Ezechias showed the envoys all his treasures.

9. Learning of this, Isaias said, "Hear the word of the Lord: 'Behold, the days shall come when all shall be carried into Babylon. Nothing shall be left.' "

Micheas

1. In the days of Isaias and Osee there lived another prophet in Juda, Micheas by name. "Woe to you that work evil!" he said when he saw how the rich abused the poor.

2. "You have coveted the fields," he cried, "and taken them by violence. You have cast out the women from the houses in which they took delight. The princes hate good and love evil, and have judged for bribes.

3. "The priests have taught for hire, the prophets divined for money. And so Jerusalem shall be as a heap of stones.

4. "But out of Bethlehem shall He come forth that is to be ruler in Israel; His going forth is from the beginning.

5. "And He shall judge among many people, and rebuke strong nations; and they shall beat their swords into ploughshares, and their spears into spades. And we will walk in the name of the Lord forever."

Josias

1. Josias, grandson of Ezechias, reigned for thirty-one years in Jerusalem. This righteous King ordered the high priest, Helcias, to have the Temple repaired.

2. In the Temple, Helcias found the Book of the Law of Moses. When it was read before the King, he tore his garments. "The wrath of the Lord is kindled against us——

3. "—for we have not done all that the Lord commands!" he cried. And Holda, the prophetess, foretold evil because the people had sacrificed to strange gods——

4. —but she said the King would not live to see it. Then Josias made a covenant with the Lord, and the people agreed to it. The idols were thrown down.

5. But Josias was slain at Mageddo when he fought Nechao, King of Egypt, who was passing through Juda with his army, to aid the Assyrians in war.

Jeremias and the fall of Juda

1. In the thirteenth year of Josias' reign, the word of the Lord came to Jeremias, a priest dwelling in a town near Jerusalem: "Whatever I command thee, thou shalt speak."

2. After Josias' death, Nechao made Joakim King of Juda and the Jews offered sacrifices to strange gods. Jeremias prophesied the Lord would destroy Jerusalem.

3. The son of the chief priest of the Temple heard Jeremias and put him in the stocks. But Jeremias said, "The Lord will give all Juda to Babylon."

4. Afterward, Jeremias called Baruch, and dictated to him the words of the Lord concerning the doom of the Jews. Baruch read the prophecies in the Temple.

5. The volume of prophecies was also read to King Joakim. But he cut it with his penknife and cast it into the fire, nor was he afraid.

6. In 597 B. C., as Jeremias had warned, King Nabuchodonosor of Babylon captured Jerusalem. He took away its treasures and its ablest people, and made Sedecias king.

7. But Sedecias revolted against Babylon. Jeremias warned the Jews that the Babylonians would retake Jerusalem.

8. "He is weakening the hands of the soldiers and the people with his words!" the princes told the King, who gave Jeremias into their hands. They let him down into a dungeon and left him to starve.

9. When an Ethiopian servant told the King, he ordered the prophet drawn up. Now he was kept in the prison courtyard.

10. Eleven years passed. In 586 B.C., Nabuchodonosor destroyed the city and freed Jeremias. Later, Jews fleeing to Egypt forced him to go along. There, for his prophecies, he was stoned to death.

In Babylon

1. Nabuchodonosor had a dream that went out of his mind but left him terrified. Nor could his wise men help. But one of the royal sons of Juda, Daniel, had been given——

2. —an understanding of dreams by God. He told the King that his dream had been of a tall statue.

3. A stone struck its feet and it broke in pieces. Then the stone became a great mountain and filled the earth. The dream meant many kingdoms would rise and fall, but at last God would set up a kingdom——

4. —that would destroy all others and stand forever. Hearing this, the King fell on his face before Daniel and said, "Verily, your God is the God of gods!"

5. Then he made Daniel governor over all his provinces, and gave high posts to his friends Sidrach, Misach, and Abdenago, also sons of the royal house of Juda.

The four in the furnace

1. Nabuchodonosor made a great idol of gold and set it up on the plain of Dura. Then he called all the chief men of Babylon to its dedication and commanded them to fall down and adore it. But Sidrach, Misach, and Abdenago would not obey.

2. In a fury, the King ordered them brought before him immediately. "If you do not adore the statue," he cried, "you shall be cast into a blazing furnace!"

3. They replied, "Behold, our God, Whom we worship, is able to save us from the furnace. We will not worship thy gods." The King told his men to bind them.

4. They were cast into the furnace—but an angel of the Lord went in with them and made the midst of the furnace like the blowing of a wind. The fire did not touch them or do them any harm.

5. "Come forth," said Nabuchodonosor, beholding this. "Blessed be your God!" And he freed them.

Ezechiel's vision

1. Ezechiel, a priest and a prophet, was among the captives carried away to Babylon. To him came visions symbolic of the doom of Old Jerusalem but also of the birth of a glorious New Jerusalem—the Church of Jesus Christ.

2. In one of his visions, Ezechiel found himself on a plain full of bones. The Lord told him, "Prophesy to these bones. Say that I will send spirit into them; I will lay sinews upon them, and flesh, and skin, and they shall know I am the Lord." And as Ezechiel prophesied, there was a noise, and the bones came together. But there was no spirit in them.

3. Then, at the Lord's command, Ezechiel said, "Come, spirit, from the four winds, and blow upon these slain, and let them live again." And they lived and stood up, an exceedingly great army. And the Lord said, "These bones are the house of Israel. I shall put My spirit in them and they shall live, and I shall make them rest upon their own land."

The writing on the wall

1. When Baltassar was King of Babylon, he made a great feast for a thousand of his nobles. They drank wine from vessels of gold and silver brought from the Temple of Jerusalem, and praised their gods.

2. Suddenly there appeared fingers as of the hand of a man, writing on the wall of the King's palace.

3. The King, in fear, cried out for his wise men. But they could not read the writing. Then the Queen said, "Let us call Daniel, who has the spirit of the holy gods in him. He will tell us the meaning."

4. Daniel said, "This is the writing: 'Mene, Mene, Tekel, Upharsin.' It means: 'God has finished thy kingdom; thou art weighed in the balance and found wanting.

5. " 'Thy kingdom is divided and given to the Medes and the Persians.' " The same night Baltassar was slain. And Darius the Mede succeeded to the kingdom.

Daniel and the lions

1. Because Daniel excelled all the other princes, King Darius thought of setting him over the whole kingdom. The princes were jealous and sought to harm him. So they persuaded the King to sign a decree.

2. It said that whoever should petition any god or man, for thirty days, would be cast to the lions. Then they watched Daniel and found him praying to his God.

3. They told the King. He tried to save Daniel, but it was the law that no decree made by the King could be altered. So Daniel was cast into the lions' den.

4. That night the King did not eat or sleep. Rising early in the morning, he went in haste to the lions' den. But Daniel was unhurt. "My God sent His angel," he said, "and shut up the mouths of the lions." Exceedingly glad, the King commanded that Daniel should be taken out, and those who had accused him were cast into the lions' den instead.

A prophet in exile

1. While in Babylon, the Hebrews drew consolation from the prophecies to be found in the later part of the Book of Isaias. For in these God proclaimed:

2. "As one whom the mother caresses, so will I comfort you." He promised that from among them would come His Servant, "despised and the most abject of men."

3. He would bear their infirmities and carry their sorrows; He would be wounded for their sins, but by His bruises they would be healed. The prophecies foretold the Lord God would gather the scattered children of Israel and they would return to a new Jerusalem. There the Church would arise, and declare the glory of the Lord.

An end to exile

1. The prophecies proved true. After the Hebrews had been in exile for fifty years, King Cyrus sent many home, and gave them the sacred vessels taken from the Temple.

2. He ordered them to rebuild the Temple of Jerusalem. But first they set up the altar and made a burnt offering to the Lord upon it, morning and evening.

3. Afterward they began to build the new Temple. When they had laid the foundations, many who had seen the old Temple wept, and many shouted for joy.

4. Now the Samaritans came. "Let us build with you," they said, "for we seek your God as you do." But the Hebrews would not let them, so they complained to the King, who halted the work. But later, when Darius was King, the building was completed. The children of Israel dedicated the Temple with joy, and offered a great sacrifice.

Queen Esther

1. In the days when Assuerus, son of Darius, reigned from India to Ethiopia, he gave a great feast for all his princes and governors in Susan, capital of his kingdom. And he commanded his chamberlains to bring in Queen Vasthi, to show her beauty to all the people. When she refused to come, the King was inflamed with fury.

2. He resolved to have another queen in place of Vasthi. Many beautiful maidens were brought before him, and he chose Esther, adopted daughter of Mardochai. She did not tell the King she was a Jewess.

3. The King's life was saved by Mardochai, who overheard two of the King's officers plotting.

4. Not long afterward, King Assuerus issued an order that everyone should bow to Aman, his favorite prince. When Mardochai refused, Aman was so angry that he decided to destroy not Mardochai alone, but all the Jews in the kingdom.

5. He persuaded the King to let him do what he would with the Jews. Then he sent out orders to kill them on a set day. When Mardochai heard, he told Esther.

6. She invited the King and Aman to a banquet. The night before, the King could not sleep, and had his chronicles read to him. He heard how Mardochai had saved him.

7. So he sent Aman to set the King's crown on the Jew's head, and to shower him with honors.

8. Now Aman had prepared a high gibbet to hang Mardochai on; but when Esther, at the banquet, told the King about Aman's plan to destroy her people, Aman was hanged on the gibbet instead.

Nehemias builds the walls

1. The cupbearer to Artaxerxes was Nehemias. One day the King asked him, "Why is thy face sad?"

2. "Why not," he answered, "seeing the walls of the city of my fathers are burnt." The King was moved, and permitted him to go and rebuild the walls of Jerusalem.

3. Captains of the army and horsemen escorted Nehemias to Jerusalem. With a few others, he went out by night and viewed the broken wall, the burnt gates.

4. "Let us rise up and build!" he told the people, and they set to work. But when the Arabians, Samaritans, and Ammonites heard, they came to fight against Jerusalem. The builders worked each with a sword in one hand, while others stood ready with spears and bows.

5. Finally the wall was finished. At its dedication, the princes of Juda marched upon the wall in procession with the priests and two large choirs that gave thanks to God. They made great sacrifices; and the joy of Jerusalem was heard far off.

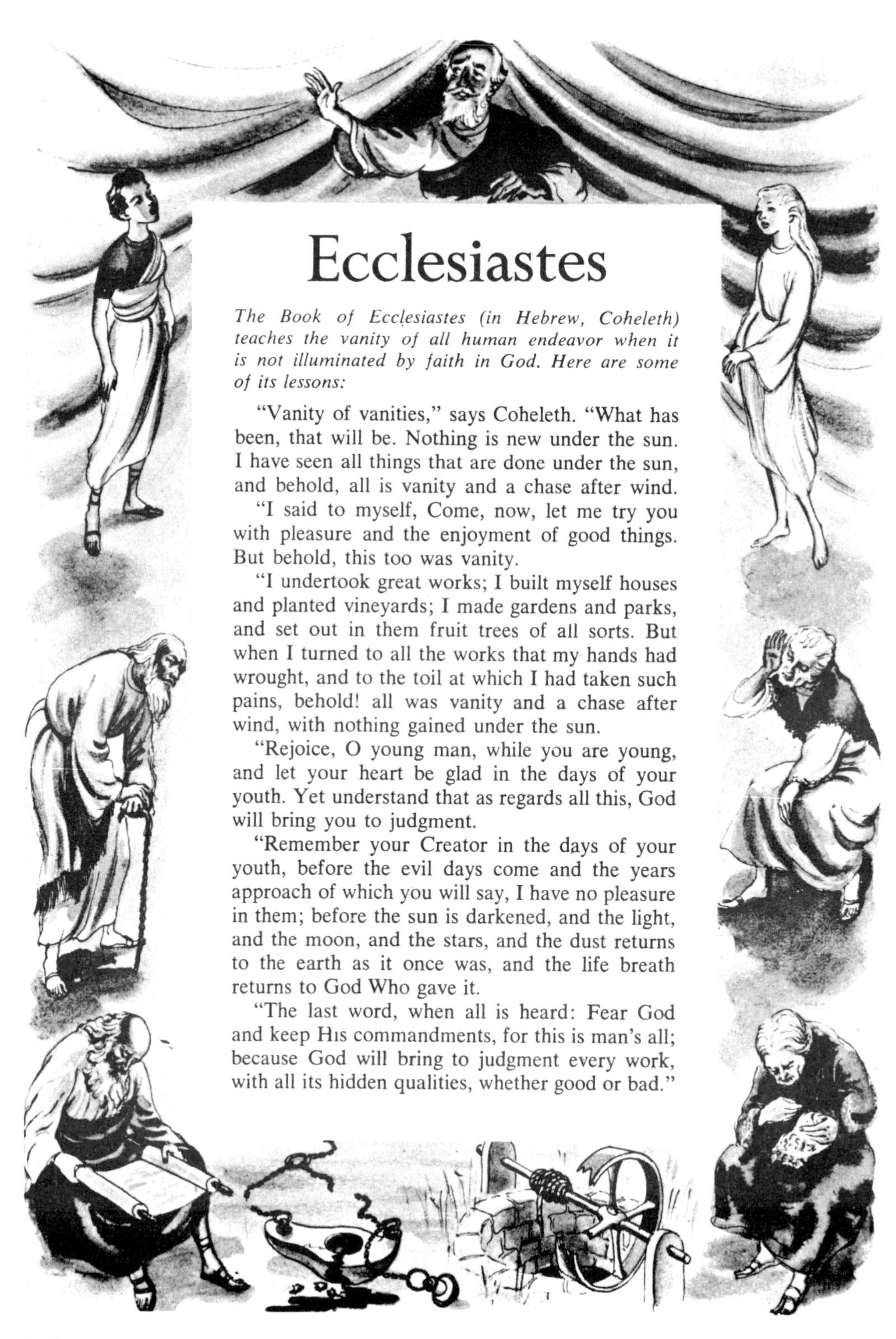

Ecclesiastes

The Book of Ecclesiastes (in Hebrew, Coheleth) teaches the vanity of all human endeavor when it is not illuminated by faith in God. Here are some of its lessons:

"Vanity of vanities," says Coheleth. "What has been, that will be. Nothing is new under the sun. I have seen all things that are done under the sun, and behold, all is vanity and a chase after wind.

"I said to myself, Come, now, let me try you with pleasure and the enjoyment of good things. But behold, this too was vanity.

"I undertook great works; I built myself houses and planted vineyards; I made gardens and parks, and set out in them fruit trees of all sorts. But when I turned to all the works that my hands had wrought, and to the toil at which I had taken such pains, behold! all was vanity and a chase after wind, with nothing gained under the sun.

"Rejoice, O young man, while you are young, and let your heart be glad in the days of your youth. Yet understand that as regards all this, God will bring you to judgment.

"Remember your Creator in the days of your youth, before the evil days come and the years approach of which you will say, I have no pleasure in them; before the sun is darkened, and the light, and the moon, and the stars, and the dust returns to the earth as it once was, and the life breath returns to God Who gave it.

"The last word, when all is heard: Fear God and keep His commandments, for this is man's all; because God will bring to judgment every work, with all its hidden qualities, whether good or bad."

The trials of Job

1. Job was an upright, God-fearing man who had a large family and great possessions. His story teaches us that man's afflictions are not always punishments for sins; rather, that the faith of the unfortunate often increases their merit before God.

2. Satan said to God, "Thou hast favored Job—but take away what he has, and surely he will blaspheme Thee." "All that he has is in thy power," the Lord answered.

3. And Job received bad news. Messengers came and told him his oxen, asses, and camels had been stolen and his servants slain; lightning had struck his sheep.

4. Another messenger arrived. "A great wind shook the house of thy eldest son, where thy children were eating—it fell on them and they are dead," he cried.

5. Job tore his garments and shaved his head. Then he fell upon the ground and worshipped God. "The Lord gave and the Lord has taken away," he said.

6. Once more God allowed Satan to test Job. He was smitten from head to foot with severe boils.

7. "Curse God and die," his wife advised. But Job said, "We accept good things from God; should we not accept evil?"

8. Hearing all the evil that had befallen him, Job's three friends, Eliphaz, Baldad, and Sophar—and a man named Eliu—came to comfort him. They sat with him seven days and spoke no word, for they saw his grief. Then they said he was being punished for some sin.

9. But even in the midst of his suffering Job found the Lord near. "I have heard of Thee by word of mouth, but now my eye has seen Thee!" he cried.

10. So the Lord gave Job twice as much as he had before, blessing the end of his life more than the beginning with possessions and sons and daughters.

Jonas

1. The word of the Lord came to Jonas, a prophet of Galilee, saying, "Arise, and go to Ninive, the great city, and preach in it, for the wickedness thereof is come up before Me." But Jonas rose up to flee from the face of the Lord.

2. Going down to Joppe, he went on board a ship bound for Tharsis. But the Lord raised a great tempest in the sea.

3. The ship was in danger of breaking up. Frightened, the mariners cried to their god for help, and cast the cargo overboard.

4. They asked Jonas to pray, too. Then, believing that the storm was a punishment for the sin of one of them, they cast lots to discover who was guilty. The lot fell upon Jonas. "Cast me into the sea," he said. "I know that for my sake this tempest is upon you." So they threw him overboard. A great fish swallowed him.

5. Jonas was in the belly of the fish three days and nights. And he prayed.

6. The Lord spoke to the fish and it vomited Jonas upon the dry land.

7. The word of the Lord came to Jonas again: "Go to Ninive and preach." So he went there. "Yet forty days, and Ninive shall be destroyed!" he cried.

8. The King of Ninive heard, and proclaimed a fast for everyone. Seeing they had turned from their evil way, God had mercy on them. But Jonas was angry.

9. For had he not proclaimed, as God ordered, the destruction of the city? Then Jonas went out of the city, made himself a hut, and sat in it, watching.

10. Ivy sheltered him. When it withered, he was upset, but the Lord said, "Thou art grieved merely for ivy—shall not I then spare Ninive, that great city?"

The Years Between

MANY and wonderful are the stories and happenings of the Old Testament. Most of the chief ones have been told, but there are still others that everyone should know. The Book of Tobias is one of these. It tells us of a holy man, Tobias, who, in the days of the captivity, remained steadfast in his faith in God, even though he became blind; as a reward, his sight was restored by God through the Angel Raphael. The Book of Judith relates the story of a heroic woman who slew the general of an enemy army and saved her people from destruction.

Four hundred years separate the Old Testament account of the rebuilding of the walls of Jerusalem by Nehemias from the first story told in the New Testament, that of the birth of Our Lord Jesus Christ.

They were four hundred years of oppression, during which the Jews clung steadfastly to their faith in God, and increasingly cherished their hope that there would come to the people a Messias, God's Anointed One, who would set them free from the tyranny of their conquerors. In these next pages something of the story of those years is told as we learn it from the First and Second Books of Machabees, with which the Old Testament closes, and from historians.

RULE OF THE GREEKS

The Persian Empire of Cyrus, Darius and Artaxerxes, which had absorbed the kingdom of Juda, fell, in its turn, to the all-conquering Greek, Alexander the Great. The Jewish historian Josephus tells us that Alexander visited Jerusalem and worshipped in the Temple.

His rule over the Jews was a friendly one; but on his death his successors fought over the country. Ptolemy Soter, one of Alexander's generals, who had taken over Egypt, invaded Palestine, seized Jerusalem, and took captive thousands of Jews, whom he transported to Alexandria.

Another of Alexander's generals, Seleucus, had become ruler of Syria on Alexander's death; and his successors, the Seleucids, wanted Palestine for themselves. Bitter battles were fought in Palestine, and the country eventually fell into the hands of the Seleucids.

OPPOSING PARTIES

Certain sections of the Jews favored the Seleucids, and sought to save their nation not by fostering its religion but by accepting its position as an important part of the Greek Empire. They asked the support of Antiochus Epiphanes, now on the Syrian throne, and he invaded Palestine because of the disturbances created by those Jews who opposed this pro-Greek section of their people.

When he reached Jerusalem, he robbed the Temple of its sacred vessels, and even took away the veil that hid the Holy of Holies. He set a Syrian guard in a tower overlooking the Temple; and, in the Temple itself, he put

Mathathias killed the Syrian officer before the heathen altar.

up an image of the pagan god, Zeus. Then he ordered that the Jewish religion should be wiped out, and the worship of pagan idols ruthlessly enforced.

It was obvious that there would be resistance by all devout Jews to this order. The lead came from an aged priest, Mathathias, in the little town of Modin, where a heathen altar had been set up. A royal Syrian officer commanded that a sacrifice should be made to show the people's acceptance of the pagan gods. Mathathias at once killed both the officer and the Jew who had been about to perform the sacrifice.

JUDAS MACHABEUS AND HIS BROTHERS

The loyal Jews united, and a mighty struggle developed. Mathathias died, but he left five sons to carry on his work. The first was Judas, called Machabeus (The Hammerer). He was victorious in many battles, and eventually won back the Temple at Jerusalem, which was cleansed and dedicated for the worship of Yahweh again. He also sent an embassy to the Roman Senate.

When at last Judas died in battle, his brother Jonathan succeeded him as the leader of the Jews and was also made high priest. The position of the Jews was not secure, but they had become powerful enough for both the King of Syria and his rival to try to win Jonathan's support. He defeated all attempts made to conquer him, but was at last treacherously slain by Tryphon, an officer of Alexander Balas, whom Jonathan had supported, and who had gained the throne of Syria.

Judas won back the Temple.

A third brother, Simon, succeeded Jonathan, and beat off Tryphon's army. Gradually, under this high priest, the Jews won more independence, peace and prosperity, and were allowed to coin their own money. Simon's death—he was murdered by his son-in-law—was a great disaster for the people; and so beloved was he that a brazen tablet was put in the Temple in his honor.

The Jews coined their own money.

THE STRUGGLE CONTINUES

Simon's son, John Hircanus, continued the struggle of the Jews and led them in successful wars against the Samaritans and the Edomites. One of his three sons, Aristobulus, took the title "King of the Jews"; he murdered his brother Antigonus, and soon afterward died himself, leaving his other brother, Alexander Jannaeus, to extend the power of the Jewish kingdom.

Alexander's widow, Alexandra, next ruled the country through the Pharisees, who were now powerful in the land, and her son, Hircanus, became high priest. Hircanus and his brother, Aristobulus II, quarreled as to who should be king, and finally it was the rich Idumean, Antipater, father of Herod the Great, who persuaded the Roman general, Pompey, to appoint Hircanus "King" and himself "Procurator" (Governor) of Judea.

THE ROMANS IN JERUSALEM

But when war between the adherents of the two brothers broke out, Pompey and his Roman legions themselves took a hand. Pompey laid siege to Jerusalem, and took the city. Once again, to the horror of the Jews, the Holy of Holies was entered. Thousands of Jews were massacred. Aristobulus and his family were taken captive, and Judea fell under the rule of Rome

Antipater was determined to have the support of the Romans, and when Pompey was killed in battle he at once transferred his allegiance to Caesar.

Pompey took Jerusalem and the Romans entered the Holy of Holies.

Caesar confirmed his position as Procurator, and that of Hircanus as high priest.

Herod, the son of Antipater, followed his father as Procurator, and went to Rome, where he was appointed by the Senate as "King of the Jews." Then, returning to Palestine, he captured Jerusalem with Roman aid, and without mercy killed all those who opposed him.

THE REIGN OF HEROD THE GREAT

In an attempt to make friends of the Jews and so strengthen his position, Herod married Mariamne, granddaughter of Hircanus II, and appointed as high priest her seventeen-year-old brother, another Aristobulus, and one of the most handsome men in Judea.

But Herod became jealous of his brother-in-law's popularity; and, it is said, when Aristobulus was bathing with other youths in the luxurious warm baths at Jericho, soldiers appeared and held him under the water until he was drowned.

Herod also murdered his wife, her two sons and another son of his. It is not surprising, therefore, that after the wise men came seeking Jesus, "He that is born King of the Jews," Herod murdered all the young children at Bethlehem.

THE TEMPLE REBUILT

But one good thing Herod the Great did for the Jews. He rebuilt the Temple with great magnificence, though only priests were allowed to do the actual building, and he himself was not allowed to set foot on the sacred soil.

As long as politics was kept separate from religion, he encouraged religion; and he managed to maintain peace throughout the country until his death.

PART III

The Story of His Church

YOU will by now have seen that the stories of the Bible are one story —the story of God seeking, through the centuries, to give men peace and goodwill on earth, and to equip them for the life of heaven.

Before He ascended, Jesus had commanded His disciples to go and preach to all nations. That they might do this work, He promised them the power of the Holy Spirit, and His own Presence—"Behold, I am with you all days," He said, "even unto the consummation of the world."

In this section, which is based on the Acts of the Apostles and the Epistles, we shall see how the promise was fulfilled, and how the Apostles obeyed this command. We shall see them traveling abroad with their good news (Gospel) and hear of the adventures that befell them. Everywhere they went, some believed and became disciples. We shall discover the strange case of the Apostle Paul, who persecuted the Christians, but, after he met the risen Lord on the Damascus road, became the "Apostle to the Gentiles," traveling throughout the world and founding Churches wherever he went. We shall see the vision which John saw, on the Island of Patmos, of Jesus seated on His heavenly throne, and innumerable followers around Him; and the Last Judgment of all earth when God, through Jesus, will end this universe, and there shall be "a new heaven and a new earth."

To complete the story of the Apostles we shall turn to other early Christian writings.

In the pages entitled "The Story Continues" you will see how wonderfully and widely the Church spread before the end of the first century.

This story of the Bible is the most significant story in the history of mankind and—the story continues. Everywhere, north, south, east and west, there are those who believe that Jesus is the World's Only Hope, the Son of God and Savior of Mankind, and who devote their lives to His service.

The story continues. You are writing it now, on the pages of history, as you think over these things and follow His guidance.

The purpose of God, of which this has been the record, is that men everywhere shall become God's sons. The coming of Jesus as Savior and the gift of His Spirit are intended for all — for "to you is the promise and to your children, and to all who are far off, even to all whom the Lord our God calls to Himself."

The upper room

1. After they had seen Jesus taken up into heaven, the apostles, with other followers of Jesus, returned to Jerusalem. They mounted to an upper room and continued steadfastly in prayer. Then Peter stood up and reminded them that Judas, who had been numbered among them, had hanged himself, and that they must choose another to take his place.

2. They put forward two: Joseph, called Barsabbas, and Matthias. And they prayed, "Lord, Who knowest the hearts of all, show which of these two Thou hast chosen." Then they drew lots. The lot fell upon Matthias, and he was numbered with the eleven apostles.

Pentecost

1. When Pentecost was drawing to a close, they were all together. Suddenly there came a sound from heaven, as of a violent wind, and tongues as of fire settled upon them.

2. They were all filled with the Holy Spirit and began to speak in foreign tongues. Now there were staying at Jerusalem devout Jews from every nation. They were bewildered because each heard the disciples speaking in his own language. But Peter, standing up with the Eleven, told the people about Jesus—His miracles, His death and His resurrection.

3. "Repent and be baptized in the name of Jesus for the forgiveness of your sins," Peter said, "and you will receive the gift of the Holy Spirit." That day about three thousand souls were baptized. They continued in the teaching of the apostles, the communion, and prayer.

At the Beautiful Gate

1. Some days later Peter and John went up into the Temple at the time of prayer.

2. At the gate called the Beautiful, a man who had been lame from birth, seeing Peter and John, asked for alms.

3. But Peter, gazing upon him with John, said, "Look at us." He looked at them earnestly. "Silver and gold I have none——

4. "—but what I have, I give thee. In the name of Jesus Christ of Nazareth, arise and walk," said Peter, and he raised him up. Immediately his feet became strong and he began leaping and praising God. The people were filled with wonder, but Peter said, "It is the faith that comes through Jesus Christ that has given him the perfect health you see."

On trial for Jesus

1. While Peter and John were speaking to the people, the priests and the officer of the Temple, and the Sadducees came. They set hands upon the apostles and placed them in custody till the next day. But many of those who had heard the Word believed.

2. On the morrow, the rulers, elders, and Scribes gathered together with Annas and Caiphas. They began to question Peter and John: "By what authority or in what name have you done this?" Peter answered, "In the name of Jesus Christ, Whom you crucified——

3. "—and Whom God raised from the dead. Neither is there salvation in any other name under heaven."

4. The Council charged them not to teach at all in the name of Jesus and, after threatening them, let them go. The apostles came to their companions and reported this. Then they prayed and were filled with the Holy Spirit.

Ananias and Sapphira

1. The believers who owned lands or houses used to sell them and lay the price at the feet of the apostles for sharing. Now Barnabas was one who did this.

2. Two others, Ananias and Sapphira, his wife, sold a piece of land and kept back part of the price. Ananias brought the rest, pretending it was all.

3. But Peter said, "Ananias, why has Satan tempted thy heart? Thou hast lied not to men, but to God." Ananias, hearing these words, fell dead.

4. The young men carried him out and buried him. Later his wife, not knowing what had happened, came in. Peter questioned her about the price of the land.

5. She, too, lied. "Those who have buried thy husband are at the door," Peter said, "and will carry thee out, too." Immediately she also fell dead.

Gamaliel's advice

1. So many wonders were done by the hands of the apostles that the sick were carried into the streets on beds so that Peter's shadow at least might fall on some of them.

2. The chief priests, jealous, seized the apostles and put them in the public prison. But during the night an angel of the Lord opened the doors of the prison, and said, "Go, speak in the Temple to the people."

3. The officers came and did not find them in the prison. Someone told the priests they were in the Temple.

4. The officers brought the apostles and set them before the Sanhedrin. "We charged you not to teach," the high priest said. Peter answered, "We must obey God rather than men." The priests, when they heard this, wanted to slay them, but Gamaliel, a teacher of the Law, said, "If it is the work of God, you will not be able to overthrow it."

The first martyr

1. As the number of the disciples was increasing, there arose a murmuring among the Greek-speaking Jews that their widows were being neglected in the daily sharing of food. Seven men were put in charge of this work. They were called deacons.

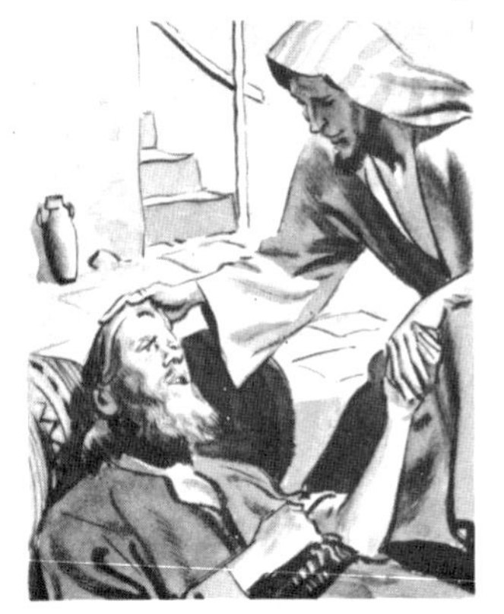

2. One of them, Stephen, was full of grace and power, and worked great wonders.

3. Some Jews from Africa and Asia, after disputing with Stephen, bribed men to say they had heard him speaking against God. He was brought before the Sanhedrin.

4. In his defense, Stephen said, "Which of the prophets have not your fathers persecuted? And you have now been the betrayers and murderers of the Just One."

5. They were cut to the heart and gnashed their teeth. But he said, "Behold, I see the heavens opened, and the Son of Man standing at the right hand of God."

6. They rushed upon him, cast him out of the city, and stoned him. And while they were stoning Stephen, he prayed, "Lord Jesus, receive my spirit." Falling on his knees, he cried out, "Lord, do not lay this sin against them." With these words he died. The witnesses laid down their garments at the feet of a young man named Saul. And Saul approved of his death.

Simon the sorcerer

1. There broke out a great persecution, and all except the apostles were scattered abroad. Philip, another deacon, went to Samaria.

2. The crowds gave heed to Philip, seeing the miracles he worked. There was great joy in the city and many were baptized. Among them was a man named Simon, who had been practicing sorcery and astounding the people of Samaria.

3. Simon attached himself to Philip; at sight of the great miracles being wrought, he was amazed.

4. The apostles sent Peter and John to the Samaritans that they might receive——

5. —the Holy Spirit. When Simon saw the apostles' power, he offered them money for their secret. "The gift of God cannot be purchased," Peter said. "Repent and pray!"

Philip and the Ethiopian

1. An angel spoke to Philip, saying, "Go south to the Gaza road." He arose and went. And behold, a minister of Candace, queen of Ethiopia, had come——

2. —to Jerusalem and was returning, sitting in his carriage and reading the prophet Isaias.

3. He asked Philip to get up and sit with him. The passage of Scripture he was reading was: "He was led like a sheep to slaughter." The minister asked, "Of whom is the prophet saying this?" Philip preached Jesus to him.

4. As they went along, they came to some water. The minister said, "What is there to prevent my being baptized?" "If thou dost believe with all thy heart, thou mayest," said Philip. "I believe," he replied, and Philip baptized him.

The conversion of Saul

1. Saul, breathing threats of slaughter against the disciples, went to the high priest and asked for letters to the synagogues of Damascus so he might arrest any there.

2. As he drew near to Damascus, suddenly a light from heaven shone round him. Falling to the ground, he heard a voice saying to him, "Saul, Saul, why dost thou persecute Me?" And he said, "Who art Thou, Lord?" "I am Jesus, Whom thou art persecuting." "Lord, what wilt Thou have me do?" asked Saul, trembling.

3. The Lord said, "Go into the city, and it will be told thee what thou must do." When Saul arose, he was blind. Leading him by the hand, his men brought him to Damascus.

4. In Damascus the Lord appeared to a disciple named Ananias and said, "Go and ask at the house of Judas for a man of Tarsus named Saul, for in a vision he has seen thee——

5. "—restoring his sight. I have chosen him to carry My name among nations."

6. So Ananias departed and entered the house. Laying his hands upon Saul, he said, "Brother Saul, the Lord has sent me that thou mayest recover thy sight——

7. "—and be filled with the Holy Spirit." And Saul recovered his sight, was baptized, and began to preach in the synagogues that Jesus is the Son of God.

Saul's escape from Damascus

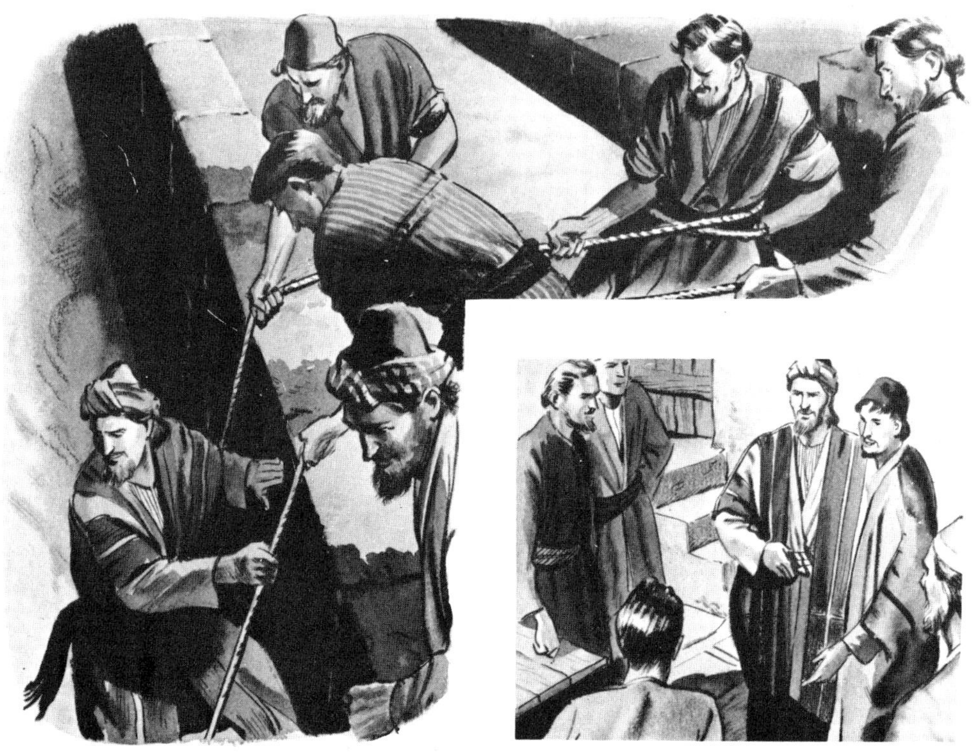

1. As time passed, the Jews made a plot to kill Saul. They were guarding the gates both day and night, but his disciples let him down over the wall in a basket.

2. On his arrival at Jerusalem the disciples were afraid of him. But Barnabas took him to the apostles and told them how he had acted in the name of Jesus.

3. And Saul moved freely in Jerusalem, acting boldly in the name of the Lord. He also disputed with the Greek Jews——

4. —but they sought to kill him. The brethren took him down to Caesarea and sent him away to Tarsus.

Miracles of Peter

1. Peter, while visiting the disciples, came to Lydda. He found there a paralytic and said to him, "Aeneas, Jesus Christ heals thee; get up." And he got up.

2. At Joppa there was a disciple named Tabitha; this woman had devoted herself to good works and acts of charity. At this time she fell ill and died.

3. The disciples sent to Peter. On his arrival, all the widows stood about him weeping and showing him the tunics and cloaks which Tabitha used to work for them.

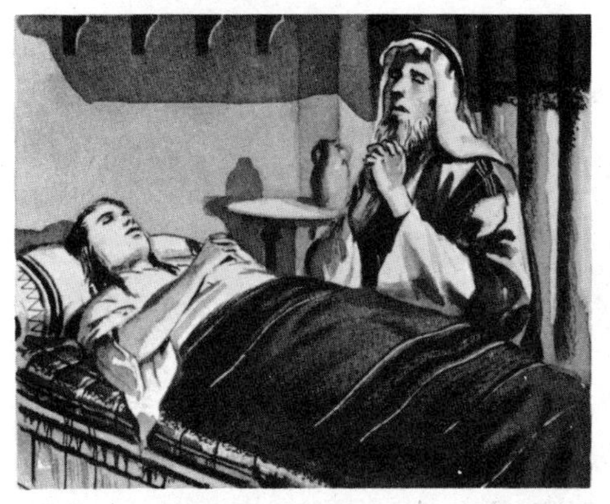

4. Peter knelt and prayed and, turning to the body, he said, "Tabitha, arise." And she opened her eyes and sat up.

5. Then, calling the disciples and the widows, he gave her back to them alive. And many believed in the Lord.

Peter and Cornelius

1. There was in Caesarea a Roman named Cornelius, a centurion devout and God-fearing. In a vision an angel of God said to him, "Send men to Joppa and fetch Peter."

2. He called two of his servants and a soldier and, after telling them the whole story, sent them to Joppa.

3. Next day, while they were drawing near the city, Peter went up to the roof to pray. He got very hungry.

4. He fell into an ecstasy, and saw a vessel coming down like a great sheet from heaven. In it were all four-footed beasts and creeping things and birds. And there came a voice: "Arise, Peter, kill and eat." But Peter said, "Never did I eat anything common or unclean." "What God has cleansed, do not thou call common," the voice answered.

5. While Peter was wondering about this, the men sent by Cornelius came.

6. They told him of Cornelius' vision. The next day he went to the Roman's house.

7. Cornelius was waiting, and Peter found many other Gentiles assembled. "We are all present to hear what has been commanded by God," Cornelius said. "Now I really understand," Peter answered, "that in every nation he who fears Him is acceptable to Him."

8. While Peter was speaking of Jesus, the Holy Spirit came upon all who were listening to his message. He ordered them to be baptized in the name of Jesus Christ.

9. When Peter went back to Jerusalem, some brethren found fault with him, saying, "Why didst thou visit the Gentiles?" He explained, and they glorified God.

"Christians"

1. Other disciples who had been dispersed by the persecution went to Antioch. Some began to preach to the Greeks, and a great number believed and turned to the Lord.

2. When this news came to Jerusalem, Barnabas was sent to Antioch.

3. There he worked among Jesus' disciples, whose number grew daily.

4. So Barnabas went to Tarsus for Saul, and brought him to help in Antioch.

5. For a whole year they took part in the meetings of the Church and taught a great multitude. And it was in Antioch that the disciples were first called Christians.

6. A prophet named Agabus revealed there would be a famine. It occurred in the reign of Claudius, and the disciples in Antioch sent relief to the brethren in Judea.

Peter's deliverance

1. At this time Herod Agrippa, the king, set hands on certain members of the Church, to persecute them. He killed James, brother of John, with the sword.

2. He also arrested Peter and cast him into prison. While Peter, bound with two chains, was sleeping between two soldiers, behold, an angel stood beside him and woke him. The chains dropped from his hands. "Gird thyself and put on thy sandals, wrap thy cloak about thee and follow me," the angel said, and Peter did so.

3. They passed through the guard and the iron gate, and the angel left him.

4. Now Peter went to the house of Mary, the mother of John Mark.

5. There many were gathered together, praying. When he knocked at the door, a maid named Rhoda came to answer it. As soon as she recognized Peter's voice——

6. —in her joy she did not open the gate but ran in and announced——

7. —that Peter was standing outside. They said, "Thou art mad!" But Peter continued knocking, and when they opened, they saw him and were amazed.

8. He related how the Lord had brought him out of the prison. "Tell this to the brethren," he said. Then he went from Judea to Caesarea and stayed there.

Saul's first missionary journey

1. Now at Antioch there were prophets and teachers, among whom were Barnabas and Saul. These two the Holy Spirit called unto His work, and the Church let them go.

2. So they, sent forth by the Holy Spirit, went from Antioch, which was the capital of Syria, to Seleucia, the seaport, and sailed to the island of Cyprus.

3. Saul and Barnabas had as assistant Mark, who wrote the gospel.

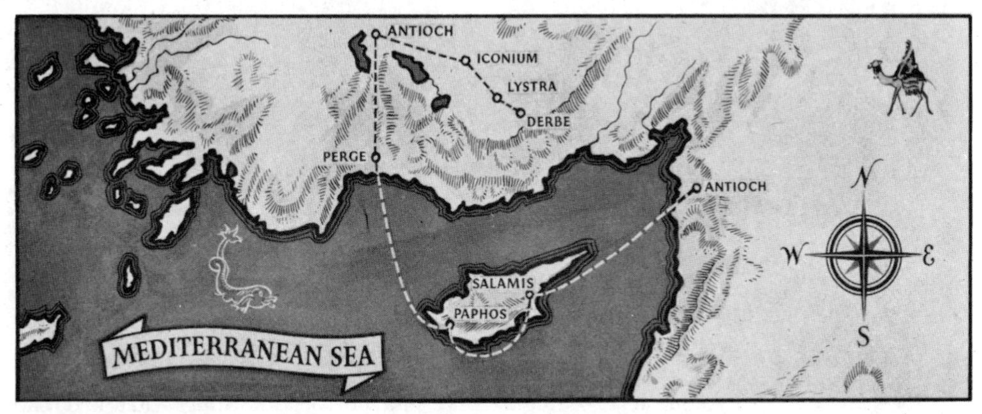

4. On Cyprus they preached through the whole island. Putting to sea from Paphos, they came to Perge. Now Mark left, and they went on to the Pisidian Antioch, Iconium, Lystra, and Derbe. Returning, they exhorted the disciples to continue in the faith. At Antioch they reported all that God had done with them, as the next pages relate.

Conversion of a Roman

1. On their arrival at Salamis, on the island of Cyprus, Saul, Barnabas, and Mark began to preach the word of God in the synagogues of the Jews.

2. At Paphos the Roman proconsul Sergius Paulus sent for Barnabas and Saul, but a false prophet, Bar-Jesus, opposed them, trying to turn the proconsul from the faith.

3. Saul, filled with the Holy Spirit, gazed at Bar-Jesus and said:

4. "Son of the devil, thou shalt be blind for a time!" Instantly there fell upon him a mist of darkness, and he groped about for someone to lead him by the hand.

5. The proconsul, seeing what had happened, believed the Lord's teaching. Then Saul (who is also called Paul) set sail for Perge with his companions.

"We turn to the Gentiles"

1. At Perge, in Pamphylia, Mark left, and returned to Jerusalem. Paul and Barnabas went on.

2. On Sabbath, in the synagogue at Antioch in Pisidia, Paul taught——

3. —that God, according to His promise, had brought to Israel a Savior, Jesus, and through Him forgiveness of sins was proclaimed.

4. Many went away with Paul and Barnabas, and the next Sabbath almost the whole city gathered to hear the two. The Jews, jealous, contradicted what Paul said.

5. "Since you reject the word of God," Paul replied, "we turn to the Gentiles." But the Jews stirred up a persecution against the apostles, so they went to Iconium.

"The gods have come"

1. At Iconium the disbelieving Jews poisoned the minds of the Gentiles against the brethren.

2. They escaped to Lystra. There a man who had been lame from birth listened to Paul. Seeing that he had faith to be cured, Paul said:

3. "Stand upright on thy feet." And the man sprang up and began to walk.

4. The crowds, seeing what Paul had done, lifted up their voices, saying, "The gods have come down to us in the likeness of men." And they called Barnabas Jupiter, and Paul Mercury (the messenger of the gods), because he was the chief speaker.

5. The priest of the temple of Jupiter brought oxen and garlands and, with the people, would have offered sacrifice to Barnabas and Paul. But the two shouted, "We are mortals! You should turn from these vain things to the living God!"

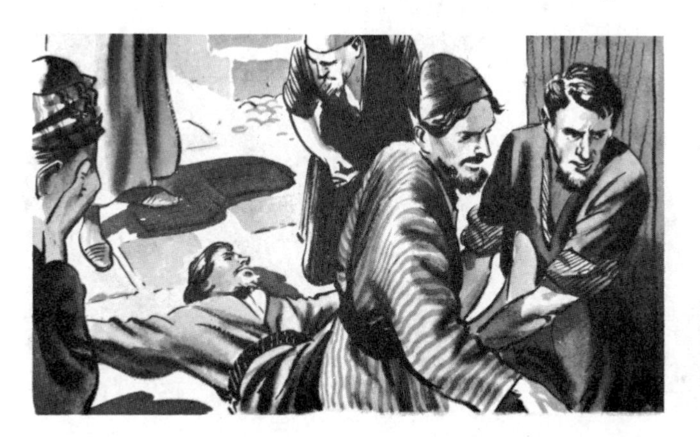

6. Some Jews arrived from Antioch and Iconium; after winning over the crowds, they stoned Paul and dragged him outside the city, thinking he was dead. But he was still alive.

7. Paul and Barnabas went on to Derbe, then back to the coast and to Antioch.

The Great Council

1. Some Jewish Christians came from Judea to Antioch and began to teach the brethren, saying, "Unless you obey the Law of Moses, you cannot be saved." No little objection was made against them by Paul and Barnabas.

2. So it was decided that Paul, Barnabas, and other disciples should go to the apostles at Jerusalem about this question.

3. At Jerusalem, some of the Pharisees who had accepted the faith said, "They must observe the Law of Moses."

4. So the apostles and elders had a meeting. After a long debate, Peter got up and said, "Brethren, why do you now try to test God by putting on the neck of the disciples a yoke which neither our fathers nor we have been able to bear?"

5. The Church decided to send a letter saying that it was not necessary for Christians to be bound by Moses' Law.

6. The bearers of the letter to Antioch were Barnabas, Paul, and two other disciples, one of whom, Silas, stayed there.

Paul's second missionary journey

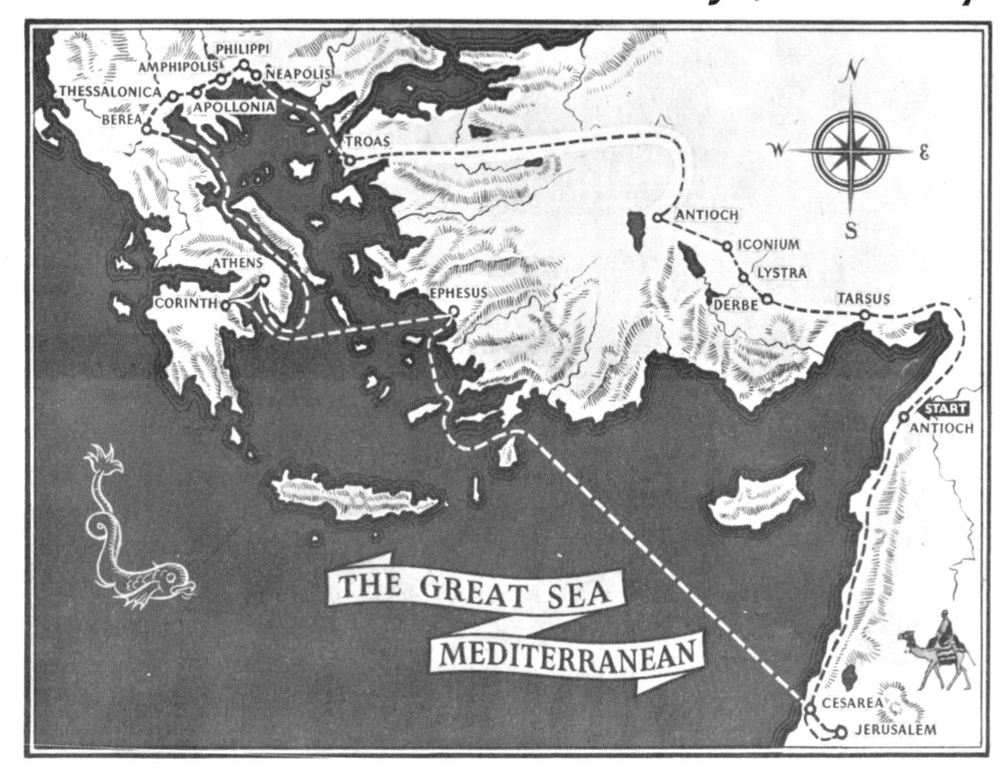

1. Paul's second missionary journey carried him into Europe. He and Silas went overland into Cilicia and Galatia, strengthening the churches he had established on the earlier journey; on to Troas; from there to Neapolis, Philippi, Thessalonica, Athens, and Corinth. Then they sailed to Ephesus, and from there back to Palestine.

2. Some time after the Council, Paul had said to Barnabas, "Let us return and visit the cities where we have preached." Barnabas wanted to take with them Mark also, but Paul disagreed, as Mark had deserted them on their first journey. A sharp quarrel sprang up.

3. So they parted. Paul, with Silas as his companion, went through Syria and Cilicia.

4. When they reached Derbe, a disciple named Timothy joined them.

5. Passing through Phrygia and the Galatian country, Paul, Silas, and Timothy were forbidden by the Holy Spirit to speak the word in the province of Asia.

6. They tried to get into Bithynia, but the Spirit of Jesus did not permit them. So they went to Troas, where Luke, a doctor from Macedonia, joined them.

7. Paul had a vision one night: a Macedonian was appealing to him, "Come over into Macedonia and save us." So they set out for Macedonia. Sailing from Troas, they ran a straight course to Samothrace, to Neapolis, and thence to Philippi.

Into Europe

1. At Philippi a woman named Lydia was listening to Paul, and the Lord touched her heart. She and her household were baptized.

2. Now a girl who possessed the divining spirit and brought her masters much profit by soothsaying, cried after Paul and Luke:

3. "These men are servants of God and proclaim a way of salvation!" Paul ordered the spirit to go out of her.

4. And it went out. Seeing their hope of profit gone, her masters seized Paul and Silas, dragged them to the market place——

5. —and accused them of teaching customs unlawful for Romans. The magistrates had them beaten and cast into prison.

6. At midnight Paul and Silas were praying. Suddenly there was a great earthquake. All the doors flew open.

7. Everyone's chains were unfastened. The jailer drew his sword to kill himself, thinking the prisoners had escaped.

8. But Paul cried, "We are all here!" The jailer ran in trembling and said, "What must I do to be saved?"

9. "Believe in Jesus," they answered. He took them to his home and washed their wounds; and he and his family were baptized.

10. When day came, the magistrates ordered them released. But Paul said, "Let them come themselves and take us out . . .

11. "We are Roman citizens, cast into prison without trial!" The magistrates begged them to leave. So they left.

"The Unknown God"

1. At Thessalonica, Paul preached that Jesus was the Messias and rose from the dead. Some believed, and joined Paul and Silas. The Jews, moved with jealousy, set the city in an uproar. A mob attacked Jason's house, where Paul and Silas were staying, but, not finding them there, dragged Jason and certain brethren before the magistrates.

2. The magistrates accepted bail and let them go. Paul and Silas went away that night.

3. At Beroea they parted, Paul going on to Athens. There he had discussions in the synagogue, and in the market place every day.

4. He told the Athenians he had seen a Greek altar with this inscription: "To the Unknown God." "What you worship in ignorance," Paul said, "that I proclaim to you. And God will judge the world by a Man Whom He has guaranteed to all by raising Him from the dead."

Tent-makers

1. After this, Paul departed from Athens and came to Corinth. There he found a certain Jew, Aquila, who had come from Italy with his wife, Priscilla, because the Emperor, Claudius, had ordered all Jews to leave Rome. Paul stayed with them and set to work, as he was of the same trade, a tent-maker. Silas and Timothy joined him.

2. In the synagogue every Sabbath, he tried to convince the Jews. But as they contradicted and blasphemed, at last he said, "Henceforth I will go to the Gentiles!"

3. So he went to live with Justus, a Gentile whose house adjoined the synagogue.

4. But Crispus, president of the synagogue, believed and so did all his household.

5. Paul lived there a year and six months. Then the Jews accused him of unlawful religious preaching. But Gallio, the Roman proconsul, dismissed them.

Paul's third missionary journey

1. Taking leave of the brethren, Paul sailed with Priscilla and Aquila to Ephesus. There he left them and put to sea again. Landing at Caesarea, he went to Jerusalem to pay his respects to the Church and then returned to Antioch.

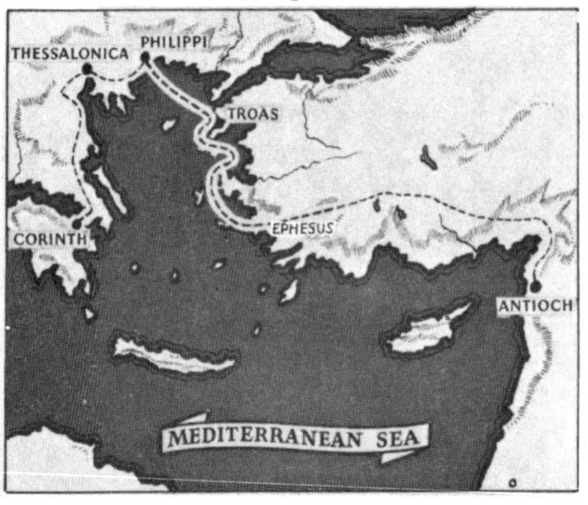

2. Afterwards, Paul traveled through the Galatian country and Phrygia, strengthening all the disciples. Now Apollos, a Jew of Alexandria, came to Ephesus.

3. He was an eloquent man, and mighty in the Scriptures, and used to teach carefully whatever had to do with Jesus, though he knew of John's baptism only.

4. Priscilla and Aquila expounded the Way of God to him. Later, in Achaia, he was of great service to those who believed.

5. Now Paul came to Ephesus and found certain disciples of John there and baptized them in the name of the Lord Jesus.

6. Paul held daily discussions in Ephesus for three years, so that all who lived in the province of Asia heard the Word. And God worked more than the usual miracles by the hand of Paul.

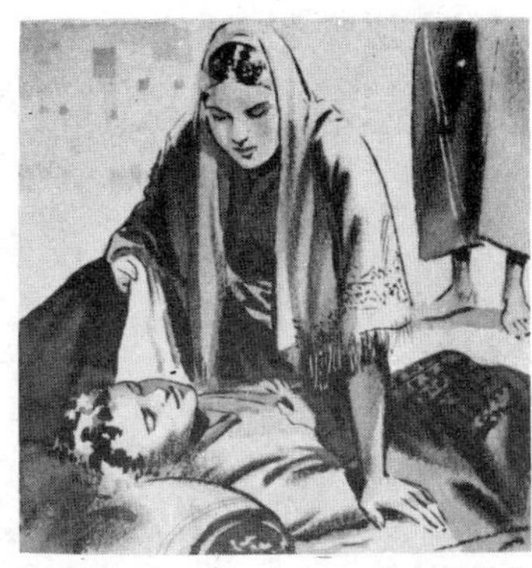

7. Even when handkerchiefs and aprons were carried from his body to the sick, the diseases left them.

8. Some Jewish sorcerers tried to imitate Paul. They attempted to invoke the name of Jesus to cure a man who had an evil spirit in him.

9. But the man answered, "Jesus I acknowledge, and Paul I know, but who are you?" And the man sprang at them with such violence that they fled.

10. When this became known, many believed, and burned their books of magic.

11. Now a silversmith named Demetrius, who made silver shrines of Diana, got together the workmen and said, "Men, our wealth comes from this trade——

12. "—and there is danger, not only that our business will be discredited because of this man Paul, but also that the temple of the great Diana will be regarded as nothing!" On hearing this, they were filled with wrath and cried out:

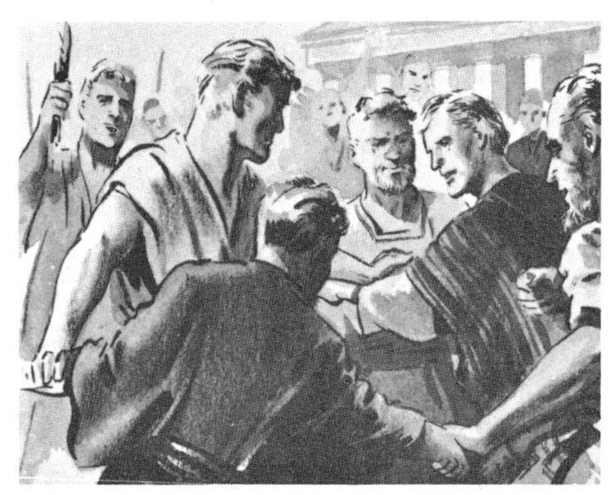

13. "Great is Diana of the Ephesians!" The city was filled with confusion. They rushed by a common impulse to the theater——

14. —dragging along two of Paul's disciples. When Paul wanted to go before the people, his friends would not let him.

15. In the theater, meanwhile, the town clerk quieted the crowd and said, "These men are neither guilty of sacrilege, nor blasphemers of your goddess. If Demetrius and the craftsmen have a complaint, let them take action on court-day."

Trouble at Corinth

1. Shortly afterwards, Paul left for Macedonia. But while he was at Ephesus, news had been brought by Apollos of trouble among the Christians at Corinth. Paul wrote them a letter, warning them not to mix with evil people; and he sent Timothy——

2. —to add weight to his advice. But reports of fresh strife reached him.

3. He heard of quarrels and evil living. "Remember only Jesus Christ," Paul wrote.

4. The news became worse, so Paul hurried across the sea to Corinth himself.

5. But they refused to hear him. In sorrow he returned to Ephesus, wrote a severe letter warning them he would return.

6. Paul was in Macedonia when Titus brought news that the Corinthians had repented. So Paul went to Corinth.

Farewells and warnings

1. Paul had planned to sail from Corinth to Palestine, to bring alms for the poor of Jerusalem and fulfill vows.

2. But a plot was laid against him by the Jews, so he resolved to return through Macedonia. He rejoined his disciples at Troas, and there they stayed seven days.

3. On Sunday, as he was to leave the next morning, Paul addressed the disciples until midnight. A young man, Eutychus, sitting at the window, was overcome with drowsiness.

4. He went to sleep and fell from the third story to the ground, and was picked up dead. But Paul went down and embraced him, and Eutychus came back to life.

5. At Miletus, Paul sent to Ephesus for the elders of the Church there. When they had come, he said, "You will not see my face again. Take care of the flock, for after my departure fierce wolves will get in among you." And there was much weeping.

6. Paul and his friends came to Caesarea, where they stayed with Philip. There, a prophet named Agabus, taking Paul's girdle, bound his own feet and hands and said, "The Jews will bind you like this at Jerusalem and deliver you to the Gentiles." "I am ready not only to be bound but even to die for the Lord Jesus," Paul answered.

7. They begged him not to go to Jerusalem, but they could not persuade him. On his arrival there, the brethren gave him a hearty welcome. The next day Paul went with his friends to James, and all the elders came in. After greeting them, he related in detail what God had done among the Gentiles through his ministry.

Paul's arrest

1. The next day Paul entered the Temple. Some Jews from Asia, seeing him, stirred up the people and seized him, shouting, "This is the man who teaches all men everywhere against our people and our Law!" The whole city was thrown into confusion. The people ran together and, seizing Paul, they proceeded to drag him out of the Temple.

2. They were trying to kill him when the news reached the commander of the Roman guard that all Jerusalem was in tumult. Taking soldiers, immediately he ran——

3. —to where the crowd was beating Paul. He seized Paul and ordered him bound with chains and taken to the barracks. Paul was actually carried by the soldiers——

4. —owing to the violence of the crowd. At the barracks steps he was allowed to speak to the people. He told them how Jesus had appeared to him and sent him to preach to the Gentiles. "Away with him!" they shouted. "It is not right that he should live!" The commander ordered Paul scourged, that he might find out why they shouted so against him.

5. When they had bound him with straps, Paul said to the centurion standing by, "Is it legal to scourge a Roman without trial?" When the centurion heard this——

6. —he went to the commander and reported. "Art thou a Roman?" the commander asked Paul. "Yes," Paul said. And the commander was alarmed.

Paul before the Sanhedrin

1. The commander ordered the Sanhedrin to assemble, and placed Paul in front of them. Paul, knowing part of them were Sadducees and part Pharisees, said, "I am a Pharisee, the son of Pharisees; it is about the resurrection that I am on trial."

2. There arose a dispute between them, for the Sadducees believed there is no resurrection and there are no angels or spirits, and the Pharisees believed in both.

3. The dispute became violent. The commander, fearing lest Paul be torn to pieces, ordered him brought to the barracks. There the Lord said to him, "Be steadfast."

4. Some Jews conspired to kill Paul when he should next appear before the Sanhedrin. Paul's nephew heard, and told him.

5. Paul sent him to the commander. At once Paul was taken to Caesarea, to be tried by the Roman governor, Felix.

Paul and Felix

1. Five days later the high priest came with some elders and Tertullus, an attorney, and presented their case against Paul.

2. Tertullus accused Paul, saying, "We have found this man a promoter of sedition and a ringleader of the Nazarene sect. He even tried to desecrate the Temple." "They cannot prove the charges," Paul answered. "I serve the God of my fathers, believing that there is to be a resurrection." Felix adjourned the trial.

3. "When the commander comes, I will decide your case," he said, and instructed the centurion to keep Paul in custody.

4. But he was allowed to see his friends. Later, Felix came with his wife to hear what Paul had to say about Jesus Christ.

"I appeal to Caesar!"

1. After two years, Felix was succeeded by Festus. The chief priests begged him to have Paul tried in Jerusalem. But Paul said, "I appeal to Caesar!"

2. Festus, after conferring with the council, answered, "Thou hast appealed to Caesar; to Caesar thou shalt go."

3. But when King Agrippa and Bernice, his sister, came to pay their respects to Festus, he laid Paul's case before the King. The next day Agrippa entered the audience hall and Paul was brought in.

4. Festus explained that Paul had done nothing deserving of death, in spite of the Jews' charges. Then Agrippa ordered Paul to speak. Paul told how he met the risen Lord on the Damascus road. "I was not disobedient to the heavenly vision," he said. "I set about declaring to both Jews and Gentiles that they should repent and turn to God."

5. Festus cried, "Paul, thy great learning is driving thee to madness!"

6. "I am not mad," said Paul, "but I speak words of sober truth."

7. Then he turned to King Agrippa. "The King knows about these things, and to him I speak without hesitation. For I am sure that none of these things escaped him, for none of them happened in a corner. Dost thou believe the prophets, King Agrippa? I know that thou dost." But Agrippa said to Paul:

8. "In a short while thou wouldst persuade me to become a Christian!" Paul answered, "I would to God that not only thou, but also all who hear me today——

9. "—might become such as I am." Later Agrippa said to Festus, "This man might have been set at liberty, if he had not appealed to Caesar."

Sailing for Rome

1. Paul, with other prisoners, was turned over to a centurion named Julius. They went on board a ship bound for the ports of Asia.

2. When they reached Myra in Lycia, the centurion found a ship bound for Italy and put them on board. With difficulty, they came to Fair Havens, in Crete.

3. Navigation was now unsafe, and Paul warned the centurion, "This voyage is threatening to bring disaster not only to the cargo and the ship, but to our lives."

4. But the centurion gave more heed to the pilot and the captain, and the majority favored sailing to Phoenis, a more secure harbor. So they weighed anchor.

5. Not long afterwards a violent wind sprang up and the ship was caught in it and driven along. With difficulty they hoisted the ship's boat aboard.

6. They used cables to undergird the ship and, afraid of being driven on the Syrtis quicksands, they lowered the mainsail. As they were being tossed about by the storm, they threw some of the cargo overboard, and the ship's gear.

7. Neither sun nor stars were visible for many days, and all hope of being saved was given up. Then Paul got up and said, "Be of good cheer; there will be no loss of life.

8. "Last night an angel told me, 'Thou must stand before Caesar; and God has granted thee all who are with thee.' I have faith it will be as has been told me."

9. The fourteenth night, the sailors began to suspect they were drawing near to some land. Taking soundings, they found twenty fathoms. A little further on——

10. —they found fifteen. Fearing that they might go on the rocks, they dropped four anchors from the stern and waited longingly for daylight.

11. Now sailors, trying to escape, lowered the ship's boat into the sea, but Paul said to the centurion, "Unless these men remain, you cannot be saved!"

12. So the soldiers cut the ropes of the boat and let her drift off. Paul begged them all to take food. He took bread and gave thanks to God before them all.

13. When day broke they noticed a bay with a beach, and proposed to run the ship ashore. The stern began to break up. The soldiers planned to kill the prisoners——

14. —lest any of them should swim ashore and escape. But the centurion, wishing to save Paul, put a stop to their plan. He ordered those who could swim to jump overboard first and get to land, and they brought the rest in, some on planks and others on various pieces from the ship.

Paul at Malta

1. All got safely to land. After their escape they learned that they had reached the shore of the island of Malta. The natives showed them no little kindness, for, because rain had set in, and cold, they kindled a fire and refreshed them all. Paul gathered a bundle of sticks and laid them on the fire.

2. A viper came out because of the heat and fastened on Paul's hand. The natives said, "Surely this man is a murderer! Though he has escaped the sea——

3. "—Justice does not let him live." But Paul shook off the creature into the fire and suffered no harm. So they said that he was a god.

4. In the vicinity there were estates belonging to the head man of the island, whose name was Publius, and he received them and entertained them hospitably for three days. The father of Publius was laid up with fever and dysentery.

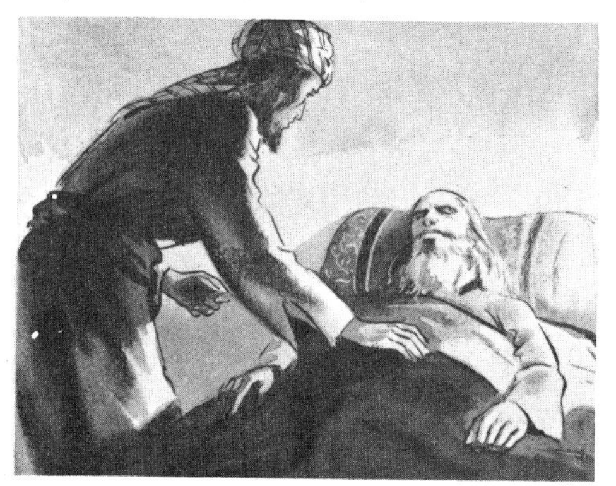

5. Paul went in and, after praying and laying his hands on him, he healed him. After this——

6. —all the sick on the island came and were cured. They honored Paul and his companions with many marks of honor.

7. The natives provided them with such things as they needed when they set sail, after three months, in an Alexandrian ship which had wintered at the island. They put in at Syracuse and stayed there three days. Then, following the coast, they reached Rhegium, in Italy.

Paul reaches Rome

1. One day later a south wind sprang up, and on the second day they arrived at Puteoli, where they found brethren. They stayed with them for seven days, then they went on to Rome. The brethren there, having had news of Paul——

2. —came as far as the Market of Appius and the "Three Taverns" to meet him. When Paul saw them, he gave thanks to God.

3. On their arrival at Rome, Paul was given permission to live by himself with a soldier to guard him.

4. Three days later he called together the leading Jews and said to them, "It is because of the hope of Israel that I am wearing this chain." He tried to convince them concerning Jesus from the Law of Moses and from the Prophets. Some believed, some disbelieved, but they could not agree among themselves.

Paul's death in Rome

1. For two years Paul lived in his house at Rome. There he welcomed all who came to him, preaching the Kingdom of God. Many among the Romans became followers of Christ, and the Church grew. Paul wrote letters of guidance to the Philippians, Ephesians, and Colossians. Then he was released and traveled to Spain and the East.

2. Visiting Crete, Paul left Titus there to organize the Church. Titus received a letter of wise counsel from him later.

3. At Ephesus, Paul left another of his missionary companions, Timothy, to take charge of the Church there.

4. Paul traveled back to Rome, where he was imprisoned a second time. Almost all of his old friends had left the city. At his first hearing, no one came to his support, but the the Lord stood by him and strengthened him.

5. In a letter to Timothy, whom he called his "beloved son," Paul revealed he was lonely, but his thoughts were only of God and the Church. "The time of my deliverance is at hand," he wrote. "Make haste to come to me. I long to see thee, that I may be filled with joy. Luke only is with me. Take Mark and bring him with thee.

6. "I have fought the good fight, I have finished the course, I have kept the faith. For the rest, there is laid up for me a crown of justice which the Lord, the just Judge, will give to me in that day." Paul was beheaded in 67 A. D.

The Revelation of St. John

At the end of the first century, John the Evangelist saw a vision of Jesus sitting on a throne in heaven, and a great multitude stood before Him. Again, he saw Jesus standing on Mount Sion, while the gospel was preached to every nation. Then John beheld Jesus on a great white throne; it was the Last Judgment, and the dead, great and small, were standing before the throne. The book of life was opened, and they were judged according

to their works, which were written in the book. Then heaven and earth passed away, and there was a new heaven and earth. And John saw a holy city, New Jerusalem, where God dwelt with men, and death was no more, nor mourning, nor crying, nor pain. And John heard God say, "I make all things new! I am the Alpha and the Omega, the beginning and the end. To him who thirsts I will give of the fountain of the water of life freely."

The Story Continues

WHAT a wonderful picture this Story of the Bible has given to us. It has spanned the ages from God's creation of the universe, through the long years of His dealings with Israel, to the coming of His Son and the first beginnings of the Christian Church. Now we have traveled as far as the Bible itself takes us. But it is not the end of the story. The establishment of the Church is the beginning of a new chapter in the annals of God's work among men. Jesus had said to His disciples: "All power in heaven and on earth has been given to Me. Go therefore, and make disciples of all nations, baptizing them in the name of the Father, and of the Son, and of the Holy Spirit; teaching them to observe all that I have commanded you; and behold, I am with you all days, even unto the consummation of the world." He had also promised them: "You shall receive power when the Holy Spirit comes upon you, and you shall be witnesses for Me in Jerusalem and in all Judea and Samaria and even to the very ends of the earth." Always, as His disciples obeyed His command, they received the fulfilment of His promise.

For the rest of the story of the Apostles we must turn to ancient writings and traditions.

PAUL AND HIS COMPANIONS

Paul, as we have already seen, at the end of the Acts of the Apostles was a prisoner in Rome.

We gather from the Pastoral Epistles and tradition, that at the end of two years he was released, and fulfilled the ambition he had mentioned in his letter to the Romans, of going westward to Spain. Clement of Rome, writing toward the end of the first century, tells of his "reaching the farthest bounds of the West"; and another old document, called the Muratorian Fragment, mentions

Peter was sentenced to death by the Roman Emperor Nero.

expressly Spain. Then, it seems he turned again to the East, revisiting Crete, where he left Titus in charge of the Church, with the responsibility of directing and expanding the Christian work there. From Crete he most probably went to Ephesus and appointed Timothy, whom he had taken as his companion on his third missionary journey, to lead the Ephesian Christians; then inland to Colossae to stay with Philemon. It would seem from his letters to Timothy that he visited Corinth, Macedonia, Miletus and Troas, and intended to spend the winter at Nicopolis, in Thrace. But he was arrested on some charge brought by Alexander, the coppersmith of Ephesus, and hurried back to Rome.

PERSECUTION OF THE CHRISTIANS

There, the Christian Church had grown rapidly; but when, in 64 A.D., a large part of Rome was burned down, the Christians had been accused of setting fire to the city and were being violently persecuted. The Emperor Nero ordered their arrest, imprisonment and death. They suffered terribly for their Faith—many were hung as living torches in the Emperor's gardens, or thrown to the lions in the Colosseum. Paul may have arrived again in Rome during this period of persecution, was tried and condemned to death. Being a Roman citizen, he was doubtless beheaded. Tradition places the site of his execution at Tre Fontane on the Ostian Way, three miles outside the city, and points to the year 67 A.D.

Many Christians were thrown to the lions.

PETER'S DEATH

Peter, meanwhile, had apparently been founding churches in North and Central Asia; but there is some reason to think that he came to Rome and was arrested and sentenced to death by Nero—probably in the same year as Paul. There is a legend that when Peter was condemned to be crucified, he cried that he was not worthy to die in the same manner as his Lord, and so was hung on a cross upside down.

Papias, Bishop of Hierapolis, writing in the early part of the second century, tells us that before his death Peter told John Mark everything that he remembered about Jesus.

Peter was the leader of the Apostles, and the Pontiff, the successor of Peter, is the leader of the Church.

"THE VERY ENDS OF THE EARTH"

We know from the Acts of the Apostles that James, the brother of John, had been killed "with the sword" by Herod Agrippa I.

The rest of the Apostles traveled far to bring the message of Jesus Christ to the world. Thomas, it is said, went to Parthia (Persia) and tradition says

It is said that Thomas reached India.

he reached India. Bartholomew, too, it has been said, went as far as India, having preached the gospel in Arabia. Matthew is said to have established himself in Ethiopia – the modern Abyssinia; while Andrew, according to tradition, preached in Scythia (the southeastern part of modern Europe, between the Carpathians and the Caucasus, Thrace and Asia Minor). He is said to have been crucified at Patras, in Achaea.

The Church historian Eusebius quotes a tradition that Thaddeus, shortly after the Ascension of Jesus, went to Edessa in Northwestern Mesopotamia, where he converted the king, Abgarus, to Christianity. Eusebius also records a tradition that Abgarus had, some years before, sent a message to Jesus, asking Him to come and heal his disease; and that Jesus had replied that He would send one of His disciples after His Ascension.

JAMES "THE JUST"

Of the other disciples, James, the cousin of Jesus, became leader of the Christians in Jerusalem. Paul, in his Epistles to the Galatians, spoke of James, Peter and John as being "the pillars" of the Church. James is said to have been so continually on his knees in the Temple that "they became as hard as a camel's." Even the Jews were filled with awe at his devotion and holiness, and named him "the Just." But during the celebrations of a Feast of the Passover, when Jewish feeling against the Christians ran high, he was thrown down from a tower of the Temple, stoned and clubbed to death.

James was continually on his knees.

MARK'S WORK

John Mark, who, as we have seen, was companion to both Peter and Paul, is said to have founded and presided over the Church at Alexandria, in Egypt; it was he who wrote the "Gospel according to St. Mark." "Mark," says Papias, "having become the interpreter of Peter, wrote down accurately everything that he remembered. Mark made no mistake, for he made it his one care not to omit anything that he heard, or to set down any false statement therein."

John used to say over and over again: "Little children, love one another."

JOHN THE APOSTLE

About the Apostle John many lovely traditions have come down to us. It is said that on one occasion, when visiting a church, he won over for Christ a youth whom he recommended for special care and training. Some years later he returned to the same place, and found that the young man had become a robber chieftain. Hearing this, John called for a horse, and himself rode off into the mountains to find him. There he begged him to return and repent. The bandit wept when he saw the beloved Apostle, and went back with him to the church where he had become a Christian. Nor would the Apostle leave him until he was fully restored.

John is reported to have taken charge of the churches in Asia, and to have been arrested during the persecution of the Christians under the Emperor Domitian. At first he was condemned to death and thrown into a cauldron of boiling oil, but by a miracle was saved, only to be exiled to the island of Patmos, in the Aegean. On his release he settled at Ephesus.

"LOVE ONE ANOTHER"

He lived to a great age; and when he was very old, tradition says, and unable any longer to preach to the people, he used to be carried into the church and repeat over and over again the words: "Little children, love one another." When he was asked why he so often repeated the words, he replied: "If this one thing were attained, it would be enough."

INDEX